By the same author:

The Liberals in Hampshire - a part(l)y history.
Part 1: Southampton 1958-65: object lessons
Part 2: Eastleigh 1965-72: out in the suburbs, something stirred!
Part 3: Eastleigh 1972-81: the thorn in the flesh bursts into flower
Part 4: Eastleigh 1978-85: a campaign in pictures - politics can be fun!
Part 5: Eastleigh 1981-90: control!
Martin Kyrle's *Little Green Nightbook*
Martin Kyrle's *Little Blue Nightbook*
Jottings from the Trans-Siberian Railway
Jottings from Russia and the Baltic States. Part 1: Russia and Estonia
A 20-20 Vision. Turning Britain into a liberal democracy

In preparation:

Jottings from Russia and the Baltic States. Part 2: Latvia, Lithuania and Finland
A Victorian Childhood

Martin Kyrle's

LITTLE ORANGE NIGHTBOOK

AUSTIN MACAULEY PUBLISHERS™

LONDON * CAMBRIDGE * NEW YORK * SHARJAH

A CIP catalogue record for this title is available from the British Library.

ISBN 9781398446991 (Paperback)
ISBN 9781398447004 (ePub e-book)

www.austinmacauley.com

First Published 2022
Austin Macauley Publishers Ltd®
1 Canada Square
Canary Wharf
London
E14 5AA

20230909

I wish to express my thanks to:

- My long-standing friend Carol Boulton, proprietor of Russell Stables in West End, Southampton, and driving force behind the Epona Trust, for reading initial drafts and suggesting adjustments.
- My oldest friend, Mike Roberts, for monitoring his recollections, six decades after the event, of our time living together in our student days, and the following year hitch-hiking the length of Norway with me but sadly without a camera. Half-a-century later with such apparatus to hand we crossed Siberia and Mongolia and a couple of years later ventured to the farthest-flung, windswept islands off the Atlantic coast of France.
- Judith Blake for her customary patience in putting this book together while enduring repeated alterations and new text or illustrations turning up just when she thought a letter had been put to bed.
- Lisa Rodrigues for editing the final draft and for her professional insights.
- And Millie Townsend for her cartoons drawn to order to put a smile on readers' faces.

Table of Contents

Introduction   9

A – on a string and a prayer   11

B – a step, back in time   17

C – and my part in the defeat of Nazi Germany   25

D – a peasant surprise   33

E – …and the band played on   41

F – la vie de bohème!   47

G – 's no joke!   57

H – on the far horizon   67

I – making the most of nothing   75

J – waving, not drowning   85

K – separate honeymoons   95

L – same options, maybe different outcomes   103

M – unloved, but not uneaten   109

N – castles in the air   115

O – world-class ruts and an uninvited guest for lunch   125

P – I cod you not!   135

Q – a scheduled trip becomes two   143

R – blackheads and black balsam   151

S – flags from the past foreshadow problems for the future   159

T – alone on the Mongolian steppe, darkness engulfed me   167

U – standing up to extremists   173

V – seeing the back of the King   181

W – twinning with a vengeance or rather, without   189

Y – be sure Ye are covered   197

Z – lost on a train in Western Bosnia   205

Epilogue: 211

The Icelandic Carthorse   212

Introduction

During the course of a long life, Martin Kyrle has done a fair bit of travelling, mostly for pleasure. Apart from crossing Mongolia after several weeks on the Trans-Siberian Railway (see inside front cover), few of the places he's visited may be classed as exotic, but catching ferries to islands off the coasts of France, Holland or Estonia or in his twenties hitch-hiking the length of Norway and coming home through Lapland has taken him to locations few people will be familiar with.

This collection of anecdotes runs alphabetically not chronologically and can be read in any order. Each letter begins with a map, an arrow and a flag offering a clue to where you're being taken. Next day, speculate where you're off to tonight. It may be with his wife fifteen years ago or with a student friend back in the 1950s long before mobile phones existed and when at every frontier passports were stamped and a different currency was needed.

The stories are designed to be read last thing at night, and the postscripts (for which, perhaps, read 'silly jokes' – but some of them entirely original!) are added just for fun to help the reader go to sleep with a smile on his or her face.

Although offered as entertainment, at times some serious analysis is woven into the narrative or an observation is made which is redolent of the times. Something, perhaps, to ponder next day while anticipating the itinerary of tonight's letter.

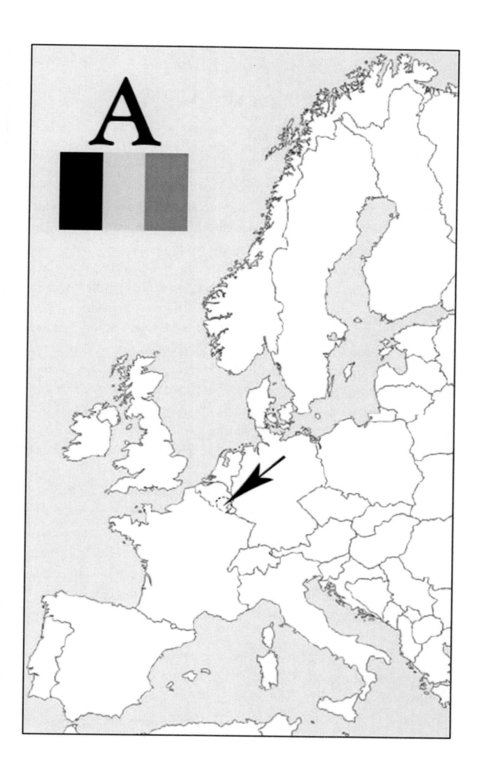

The Ardennes
On A String and A Prayer

[Conversations in italics were in French]

In the long vac I'd made my detour home from Frankfurt through Luxembourg for no other reason than that I'd never been to the Grand Duchy and wanted to tick it off the list of countries I'd visited while the opportunity offered. I'd hitch-hiked across it and been dropped in open country near the Franco-Belgian frontier. In the distance I could see the border sentry box where a solitary frontier policeman whiled away his time in a deserted post which hardly anyone ever used, except locals. He might see a genuine foreigner as a welcome novelty.

The trouble was, I'd just spent three weeks in Moscow and had got used to speaking Russian when not speaking English. I'd spent the last week in Frankfurt visiting Steffi, my German girlfriend at that time, where the language in the street was German – a language I'd never studied but had of necessity to get by in when I was on my own during the day when she was at work. Now I was in francophone country. Despite having finished with an A level at school, in the six years since leaving I hadn't spoken any French. In fact, I couldn't remember a single word!

To my chagrin to this day, what I do remember is reaching the border post, proffering my English passport to a Belgian policeman on the French frontier and saying *'Dankerschön'* when, without bothering to stamp it, he handed it back. What he must have thought of such a response I dare not imagine and I tramped off into his country without daring to look back, just in case he decided to run me in for *lèse majesté* or taking the piss. Getting through Belgium from bottom right to top left was going to be extremely embarrassing if I couldn't remember any French.

Hitch-hiking in this remote rural area was not likely to be easy, but after an hour or so of being ignored by what few cars there were, a motorcyclist on a 125cc BSA Bantam stopped and indicated that I should get up on his pillion. I'd actually had a 'Beezer Bant' myself when I was a student; my first leg up from a pushbike, the move, as a fellow student whimsically put it at the time, to hydraulic from man-draulic.

A 125cc was quite a small model for someone of my size and I remember once taking a spin out into the New Forest with a rather plump girlfriend on the back and finding to my embarrassment that the bike couldn't maintain momentum up an incline. I had to mumble some rubbish about carburettors, spark plugs and having new widgets on the sprangle docket and ask her to get off and walk that bit. A gentleman could hardly say to his lady-friend, "The bike can't make it with both of us because you're too fat!"

The rider was quite a little chap and if I got on the back with my rucksack;
(a) the machine would be seriously overloaded and
(b) he'd have so much excess weight on the back I wondered if the front wheels would stay on the ground.

The Ardennes is a hilly region with twisty roads, and he'd have his work cut out keeping his balance and the slightest error if he failed to allow for the extra weight and a misplaced centre of gravity would land us in a ditch or, the possibility crossed my mind, down an embankment and into some river a hundred feet below. To add to my worries, several parts of the frame of his machine were held together with string!

With as much grace as I could muster, I decided to decline his kind offer. But he insisted, wouldn't take no for an answer and I ended up going twenty miles perched on the pillion as he whizzed along whistling cheerfully before depositing me with a flourish and a handshake in the main square in the middle of Arlon. Grateful as I was for the ride, it'd been a nightmare. But at least the adrenalin had brought back the glimmerings of my French and I was able to thank him in the correct language, even if only just.

Out of Arlon I was picked up by a lady with her handicapped little boy in the passenger seat, who asked me to get in the back. I tried to explain that I couldn't manage much French, but that I could understand her if she spoke slowly. She asked me, slowly, where I'd come from.

"The youth festival in Moscow."

"Where are you heading?"

"Back to England."

We reached Bastogne.

Thumbing again, the next car to stop was being driven pell-mell, ground to a halt in a cloud of dust and I ran up to see if it'd stopped to pick me up or because its engine had stalled. No, it had stopped for me. The reason I hadn't expected it to stop was that it had a Luxembourg number plate and Luxembourgers had a reputation for not stopping for hitch-hikers. The reason this one had stopped was that the driver had an Italian girl as his companion. *She* had told him to stop.

Further along the road we stopped again to pick up another hitch-hiker. He proved to be German. Then a French lad. It was getting like the United Nations in the back and decidedly up close and personal: a Luxembourger driving, his Italian girlfriend – who told us her name was Lavinia – and passengers from England, France and Germany; no common language but all glad of the lift. We were all particularly relieved when Lavinia announced that instead of going to Brussels our driver would by-pass it and drop us off in Ghent. Anyone who's ever hitch-hiked knows that big towns and cities are a real bugger, because you can't hitch in a built-up area but have to somehow get yourself out into the suburbs or better still out of town altogether. To get out you have to take a bus, and that costs money. When we parted, Lavinia gave me her address in Rome and we exchanged a few letters over the next year or so.

Having to explain to my motorcyclist friend on the road to Arlon – albeit shouting in his ear from my perch on his pillion – that I'd just been to Moscow to the World Festival of Youth and Students and then down to Frankfurt to visit my girlfriend, then repeating all this to Lavinia and then in succession, making conversation with each new arrival in her car, had done wonders for my deeply interred French. Each person I spoke to corrected a different bit and I ended up with the whole account more or less word perfect. A night in the youth hostel in Ghent and having to check in with the warden brought a lot more of it back.

Now for the interesting bit and why I remember this trip so clearly. Hitching from Ghent to Bruges, I was picked up by a monk. I didn't know that monks drove cars, but we live and learn. We chatted merrily in French about who I was, where I'd been and so on. Then he asked me where I was going.

"England."

"Why?"

"I live there."

"But you're not English!"

"I am."

"Oh. I thought you were French."

He wasn't being polite. He meant it. Perhaps as he was a Flemish speaker, my French sounded to him like the French they speak in some provincial part of France, rather than what they speak in Belgium. I rapidly explained that what I'd been telling him about Moscow, Frankfurt and all the rest of it was what I'd been saying for the past three days to every driver who'd been kind enough to pick me up and that in the course of repetition and correction I'd got it off pat. Change the subject, start discussing the price of carrots, and I'd be stuck.

But I used this first-hand experience many times in my subsequent career as, *inter alia*, a teacher of Russian. To whit: if you are properly and thoroughly taught a language you never totally forget it. If you've had the grammar drummed into you, and you've learned it all by heart and had tests in class and exams and all that, it lies deep in the recesses of your memory and if you are ever in a situation where you need it again for survival it will come back.

I used to put it to my class like this: "You're learning Russian verbs, declensions, irregular nouns and all the rest of it. You can't hold much of a conversation, because you haven't reached that stage yet. But you know the grammar, how Russian works and if I give you a word you know what part of speech it is – noun, verb, adjective – how to make it agree if necessary in number and gender, put it in the past tense, in the instrumental case or in the plural as the case may be. If you go to work for an employer and suddenly he gets a letter from St Petersburg asking him to quote to supply whatever it is your firm makes, you'll be the only person on the premises who can even read it, let alone translate it. You'll find that you can, and your value to that firm is assured because you have a specialist knowledge that no one else has – and the two, three or four years you spent years ago under the cosh in my lessons worked and have paid off."

Reader: let me ask you this: What has been your experience with languages? Is it yonks since you learned them at school? Have you forgotten it all? Are you sure? What happens when you get off the ferry at Calais and need petrol and some sweets from the cashier and have to speak French for the first time since you went on holiday twelve months ago?

September 1957

Postscript

Q: If you wanted to audition fleas for a flea circus, to assess how well they could jump, turn somersaults and so on, how would you do it?

A: You would ask someone with experience of training gymnasts to carry out a fleasibility study.

Goodnight.

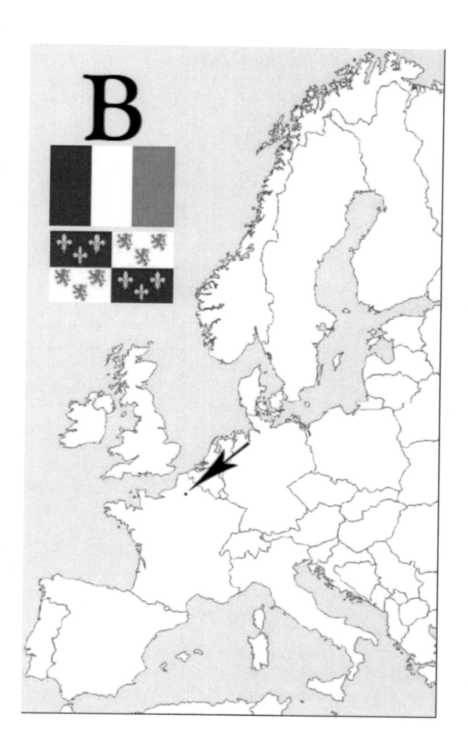

Beauvais
A Step, Back in Time

My wife Margaret and I were heading to Reims to see the royal chapels, but had planned an overnight stop. We got a bit lost driving in the middle of the town trying to find our hotel, but there it was on the corner so I turned left into the side street and luckily found a parking space straightaway. I got out of the car and as I did so a family crossed the road at the far end, two adults and a little boy. So? Dressed in medieval costume! I did a double take. On arrival in France I'd put my watch forward 60 minutes. In Beauvais, it seemed I should have put it back six centuries.

Still wondering what was going on, we got our cases out of the boot and went into the hotel. No, we didn't. It was firmly shut. A notice on the door said 'Closed until six o'clock'. Back to the car, luggage back in the boot.

"Let's go and have a look around, find a café and tread water till the magic hour when our hotel opens its doors," I said.

The distant sound of music. Not modern music, medieval. Let's head towards it and see what's going on. A few yards further along we found ourselves in the main square. Before us stood in all its splendour a magnificent Hôtel de Ville, the steps leading up to the entrance doors laid out in banks of seating and in the square a circle of people at least fifty metres across had formed (the circle, not the people). Some were in medieval costume and some not, but all being instructed over a microphone how to perform the steps of a round dance. It was very elementary: basically, three steps left, hop, three steps right, hop and repeat in time to the music. We'd stumbled on a pageant. It appeared that Beauvais was celebrating its local hero (in fact, a heroine, it soon transpired) and a *fête médiévale* was in full swing.

What luck! We'd enjoyed the similarly medieval Fête de la Scie in Harfleur on a number of occasions and coming to Beauvais for just one night to break our journey had by sheer chance picked the weekend when they were staging their equivalent.

We knew about Beauvais' claim to fame, or rather in-fame. At the trial of Joan of Arc on a charge of witchcraft, the prosecutor who condemned her to death was the bishop at the time. All the subsequent bishops had felt obliged to do their best to live him down.

The fête was extremely well planned. The musicians in the square, playing for the round dance, were also playing medieval music for entertainment. They were all dressed for the part and the instruments were good reproductions attempting to produce the authentic sound. Elsewhere were all manner of 'medieval' folk selling food and drink, demonstrating the making of arms and armour and including several dodgy characters who looked likely to cut your purse, or even your throat given half a chance.

Having bought a fifteenth century snack consisting of a slice of roast meat served on a hunk of bread at an open-air stall, we sat on a bale of straw and placed our wooden platters on another bale. Street performers including jugglers and fire-eaters demonstrated their skills for the amusement of diners and onlookers were expected to reward them by throwing them a silver piece (alright, have it your own way – a euro).

Enjoying a medieval snack in the shadow of the cathedral.

A fire-eater and other medieval performers.

The excuse for the event was to celebrate the local heroine, Jeanne Laisné, who when, in 1472, the town was besieged by Charles the Bold, Duke of Burgundy, inspired the women of Beauvais to join in the town's defence. The garrison consisted of only 300 men-at-arms and when a Burgundian soldier succeeded in planting a flag on the ramparts the fall of the town appeared imminent. At this point Jeanne, wielding an axe, fell upon him, threw him into the moat and rallied the troops. The King of France, Louis XI, was so delighted that her audacity had prevented the fall of the town that he allowed her to marry her sweetheart, loaded the couple with favours and granted numerous privileges to the townspeople which were usually the prerogative of nobles – such as the right to wear jewellery.

In my view, to justify spending money putting on a medieval festival you need an excuse, so you trawl through your local history and come up with a hero or heroine in some long-forgotten war to provide you with the pretext you need. No disrespect – I'm sure Jeanne was a patriotic woman whose memory is worth preserving. What's disputable is whether she had much contemporary fame beyond Beauvais and its surrounding villages.

She was honoured as 'Jeanne la Hachette' – 'Joan the Axe' – and a statue stands in the main square in front of the Hôtel de Ville. An annual procession is held in the town in the last weekend in June in which the townspeople dress in the costume of the period and women take precedence over men. Of course, we'd never heard of her – and I wonder to what extent that's true of French people living in distant parts of the country. She was, after all, a local heroine not a national one and the wars between the Kings of France and the Dukes of Burgundy are long past and long forgotten.

It so happens that Burgundy ceased to exist as an independent duchy after Charles' death in 1477 without a male heir when he was killed in the Battle of Nancy. Without a duke to hold them together, his disparate landholdings scattered between Switzerland and the Low Countries disintegrated and were split up and, in most instances, ended up under the control of either the King of France or the Holy Roman Emperor.

Where the frontier should truly lie between the French-speaking lands to the west and the German-speaking lands to the east remained in dispute – and the cause of much warfare – for two centuries following Charles' death. The German annexation of Alsace and Lorraine following the Franco-Prussian War in 1870–1 shows that well into the nineteenth century the question was still unresolved. The modern frontier was fixed after the First World War under the terms of the Treaty of Versailles and now that France and Germany are part of the Schengen Agreement with frontiers virtually abolished it's no longer a matter of contention.

'Twas not ever thus! The scores of castles whose ruins are to be seen all over what is now eastern France were built at enormous expense in money and labour for reasons of defence or to cow the local populace. Being gawped at by twenty-first century tourists wasn't one of them. But now – *vive la fête!*

What we particularly enjoyed was that so many townspeople had taken the trouble to dress in costume and the town council had gone out of its way to set up suitable street decorations and clear the way for the performers and those giving demonstrations. A blacksmith forging armour or a vintner dispensing medieval drink straight from the barrel needs space and not to be sharing his pitch with a sign saying 'bus stop' or 'keep left'. Modern street furniture needs to be removed or effectively masked if you're going to create anything like an authentic atmosphere. Using the side of the cathedral as a backdrop was an inspired move, too.

The one thing they couldn't provide was the overpowering stench of sweat, bodies, wood smoke, dung and rotting food which would have been normal in a medieval town – but maybe the twenty-first century health authorities won't quite permit the council to go that far.

Imagine: 'I was in Beauvais for their fête and it was really authentic – a cutpurse (a medieval pickpocket) was branded and three tourists died of the Black Death. Next year they're going to hang someone for stealing a sheep – live on TV!' Not.

The following morning prior to departure *en route* to our actual destination – Reims – we stopped off at the cathedral to see inside. The previous evening, we had eaten *al fresco* with hundreds of other locals and visitors sitting on bales of straw, watching the performers and the artisans forging metal in their fires and so on – yet there wasn't a speck of debris to be seen! How had they cleared up so quickly and so completely? I don't know – but the fact was that they had. One would never have known that the fête had ever taken place, let alone just the day before.

The cathedral had a chequered history. The story goes that in the early Middle Ages the clergy tried to ignore architectural advice in demanding that masons build in the new Gothic style. They overreached themselves, with the result that it took twenty-five years to get the choir vault up to the height they wanted in order to make it the highest in Europe and a mere twenty years more for it to fall down. Pride comes before a... What's most interesting inside are the two astronomical clocks, one fourteenth century and one dating from the mid-nineteenth.

The oldest working clock in Europe.

If you're ever overcome by an attack of the terpsichoreans then I recommend a medieval weekend in Beauvais. And don't forget the doublet and hose. Chance to buy a new hauberk to replace that old one you can no longer get into, too.

June 2002

Postscript

"I hear your brother is having health problems?"
"Yes. When he goes to France on holiday, he keeps wetting himself."
"Why's that?"
"He says it's because he's in continent."

Goodnight.

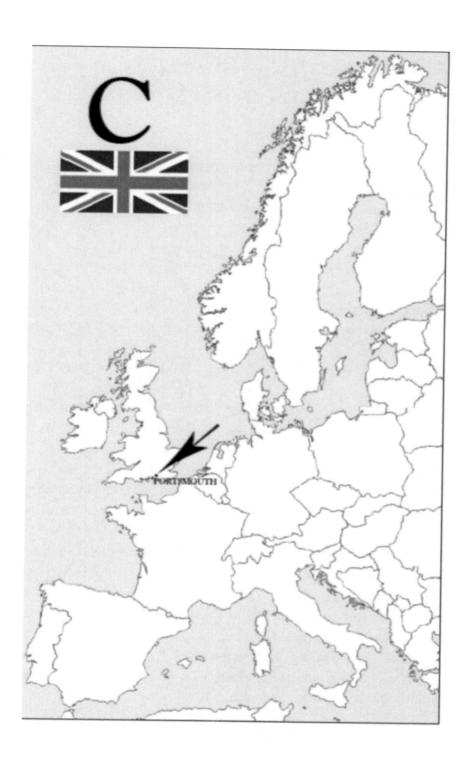

PORTSMOUTH

Clanfield

And My Part in The Defeat of Nazi Germany

Most of us nowadays live in brick houses with a slate or tiled roof, an indoor flush lavatory, running hot water, central heating and double glazing. Some householders (me included) even have solar panels, photovoltaic cells on their roofs and an air-to-water heat pump. My childhood home – believe it or not – had not a single one of these attributes. Not even brick walls.

In 1923 my grandparents bought a plot of ground half a mile along an unmade lane running along a valley floor which was at right angles to a steep hill. Approaching the very top, it was so steep that anyone who could cycle the whole quarter mile without getting off assumed bragging rights. At this junction on the main London-Portsmouth road (the A3) was a bus stop called Snell's Corner, over a mile from Horndean one way and the village centre of Clanfield the other.

There my grandparents proceeded to build their own house. For foundations, they used railway sleepers instead of concrete, somehow man-handling them one at a time on a wheelbarrow down from the main road and along the lane. Then, using corrugated iron and plywood, they constructed a building shaped like a Swiss chalet (hence the house's name – The Chalet). My grandmother was a sprightly 36 at the time, but my step-grandfather, a retired Chief ERA (Engine Room Artificer) in the Royal Navy, was 63. The house stood until the 1990s, when it was demolished to make way for a new housing development.

This was my home from the age of three until I was called up for national service at 19. The reason I was brought up by my grandparents was that my parents had divorced and my mother, unable to look after a toddler and earn a living at the same time (not easy for a young divorced woman in the 1930s) asked her mother to take me in. My grandmother – 'Nan' – agreed on condition that my mother severed all contact with me and as a result I had no contact with her again until I was 15 (which is another story!).

The shortcomings of having a house built of such materials as I've described were brought home to us in spades in the winter of 1947, when I was 14 years old and was now, as Pa Stewart had died the previous August, 'the man of the house'. Snow covered Britain for two months from late January and there were record low temperatures not matched until 1963. Having walls and a roof of corrugated iron, heat poured out of the house and warm air in a room would condense overnight on the single thickness glass windows and form ice on the inside.

Our front garden was 400 feet long, and not surprisingly our pipe from the mains water supply froze, not having been sunk deep enough. Our only source of water was for me to go outside and shovel up some snow and bring it indoors in a bucket and melt it on top of the oil stove.

Nan and I slept in the same bed with a sheet and bolster between us for decency, and we used to partly heat it by putting the cat in. When he'd warmed it up we'd take him out, still fast asleep and entirely circular, stroking him all the time and murmuring "nice pussy, nice Tibby!" so that he didn't realise what was happening – lulling him, as they say, into a false sense of security – and put him back on top of the bed lower down, where he'd carry on sleeping, still in a circle with his tail over his nose, and carry on the good work of helping us to keep us warm by keeping the bed clothes down with his weight (he was a very big tabby pussy).

We heated the bedroom with a paraffin stove, which we would carry through the house to the kitchen when Nan cooked a meal, then either eat it there or carry it back to the bedroom along with the stove. We had to make sure our coal lasted, as there was no way the coalman would be able to bring us any more and I had to go up into our little woods (our garden was an acre and a half and included a small wooded strip right across the plot two-thirds of the way up). I had to find suitable wood and saw it up into logs and chop some up for kindling.

Then there was the problem of maintaining fresh water for our three chickens and three ducks, who refused to venture out of their respective houses and whose drinking bowls had to be thawed out and replenished two or three times a day with a boiling kettle from the kitchen poured onto the ice in their bowls. But in that freeze-up we needed their eggs more than ever. Our lavatory was a bucket in the outhouse, which normally I emptied at the weekend by digging a hole somewhere in the garden, tipping the contents in and covering it up with earth. The only way I could do this during the 'deep freeze' was to take a pickaxe and do my best to dig some sort of shallow trench and hope for the best.

A last word about the freeze-up. During the two months of low temperatures and high snowfall we had no buses and if I wanted to get to school at Purbrook, seven miles away, the buses which normally ran from Portsmouth to Petersfield could only get as far as Horndean and I had to walk there to get to school and then get off there on the way back and walk the rest of the way home. Regardless of the weather I had to get to school if I possibly could, as I was due to sit for my school certificate in the summer and the direction of one's entire future depended on success in this examination. This may also be the place to tell you something about the impact of the War on us in our rural semi-isolation.

In the back garden one of our neighbours dug us an air raid shelter, which we entered down some steps and which Pa, with my help as he was now in his eighties, lined with planks and topped off with corrugated iron on top of which we placed turf – partly for camouflage and partly to improve insulation. We moved a chest of drawers in, which Nan filled with emergency supplies: dried or tinned food, bottles of water, candles, matches, spare clothes and bedding. We kept two hurricane lamps there, with a supply of paraffin oil and a stove, then moved in a couple of camp beds (we only had two) and a folding table and some deck chairs which normally we deployed in the garden during the summer.

When the siren went, warning us of a German air raid, we'd grab our dressing gowns and slippers or shoes if they were handy and leg it to the shelter, shutting the door behind us and bedding down on the camp beds and try to get back to sleep. Being only a little boy, I preferred to sit outside wrapped in my school overcoat to watch the light display in the sky created by searchlights seeking out enemy bombers, whose target was not, of course, us deep in the countryside but the Dockyard in Portsmouth twelve miles away.

Only one house anywhere near us got bombed. This was a small bungalow in a large garden and at least a hundred yards from the nearest other dwelling which got a direct hit from an incendiary bomb and burned to the ground. It was directly in front of our house about halfway up the hillside opposite so in full view and was reached by a zigzag path between fields which I used every day on my way to the main road to catch the bus to school. The occupants were two elderly spinster sisters, the Misses White, who were fortunately in their own air raid shelter in the back garden when the bomb dropped and so didn't suffer any personal injury – although they lost their home and all their possessions. As they were also my Sunday School teachers, I think this was the first time in my life that I questioned the existence of God.

Us boys used to go hunting in fields and especially up on Windmill Hill after air raids to see what debris from the previous night's raid we could find. Spent bullets of shiny, golden copper were swapped all around the playground at school and pieces of bomb casings were highly prized as trophies. One unfortunate boy found a piece of bomb which unbeknown to him hadn't fully exploded – and when he picked it up it blew his hand off. We'd all been warned about such dangers, but I'm afraid it hadn't stopped us. All part of youthful bravado and taking risks, I suppose.

One day I was up at the top of the garden when I discovered the almost impenetrable hedge between us and the adjacent field was full of soldiers – camping out in my hedge! They greeted me in a friendly fashion and asked me if I could get them some hot water so that they could have a brew-up. I said I could and shot off back down the garden.

"Nan! There's lots of soldiers all camped out in our hedge up the other side of our woods! Did you know?"

Of course, she didn't. But I got her to put the kettle on and then took it up to the soldiers who proceeded to fill their enamel mugs. We chatted, and it was obvious that they were there for a reason but had no idea what it was. Maybe Mr Churchill had got wind of a German landing to try to destroy Portsmouth Dockyard and they were being deployed to repulse the invaders? They were just 'obeying orders'.

Nan, my grandmother. Ada Amy Stewart (1887–1958)

A couple of days later they'd all disappeared as suddenly as they'd arrived. The news on the radio that evening revealed all.

Those soldiers hadn't been camping out in my hedge ready for a possible German invasion but the precise opposite: they'd been moved there to be ready for embarkation for the landings in Normandy on D-Day.

If anyone asks me, "What did you do in the War?" not realising that despite being old I'm not quite old enough to have taken part, I say: "I made tea for some soldiers before they went off to take part in the D-Day landings." Which is true – I really did! Though, of course, I didn't realise that at the time and I don't think I qualify for the defence medal.

June 1944

Postscript

First small boy: "Gosh! It's so hot today! I feel like an ice cream."
Second small boy: "That's interesting. What does an ice cream feel like?"

Goodnight.

Desyatnikovo*
A Peasant Surprise

[Conversations in italics were in Russian]

When Mike and I decided to spend a month crossing Siberia on the railway, most people's reaction was "Innit cold?"

To which invariably I replied, "Yes, in winter. We're going in September. It should be in the 20s."

On the far side of Lake Baikal in Eastern Siberia lies Ulan Ude* the capital of the Buryat* Republic. The tsars and the communists who followed them encouraged Russians from the west to settle in the east, offering inducements such as free land for farmers and higher pay for other workers. As a result, the majority of the people living in Siberia's main towns and cities are in fact ethnic Russians.

It's a very fine city, and there seems to be no tension between the people despite the indigenous Buryats being a minority, only 20%, in their own capital. No doubt the reason is that they have become thoroughly assimilated and all speak Russian. The city centre is dominated by the Parliament and other public buildings, and nearby are some grand concert halls and comfortable hotels built in classical style. Prominent in the main square is a monumental head of Lenin, said to be the largest in Russia.

In most parts of the country statues of the Bolshevik leader have been removed as Russia deliberately tries to distance itself from the dark communist period in its history – as has also happened in other countries formerly part of the Soviet bloc. Against the odds, Lenin continues to dominate the main square in the Buryat capital because newlyweds like to pose in front of him and then gather the rest of their wedding guests around them and take even more photos. The head is a unique back-drop! As we stood watching while one wedding group dispersed, the next lot who'd been waiting by their cars out of shot moved in and assumed their poses, and the process repeated itself. Mike busied himself taking his own photos of successive groups.

Our programme for the next day began with Ala*, our Buryat guide, taking us by car on a visit to Ivolginsk*, the centre of Buddhism in Russia and renowned for the variety and opulence of its datsans, or seminaries. But that's for another time. We left the colourful stupas with their relics, ashes and offerings and drove into the countryside for an hour to see what sort of welcome we'd get from the peasant women of Desyatnikovo.

Meantime, we seemed to have picked up some more tourists – we were being followed by another car! It turned out two middle-aged ladies from London who were staying at our hotel had also booked this excursion with another guide and had now caught up with us.

The village appeared pretty run-down and even more so as we left the main road and headed between the wooden houses to a back street and turned left along a bumpy track. It became clear which house was our destination, as a welcoming party comprising four ladies in traditional peasant costume was lined up outside the garden gate to greet us. Some appeared to be quite elderly – not as elderly as me, so I don't think I'm being unchivalrous in so describing them.

The shortest one introduced herself as Galina. She had a weather-beaten peasant's face but spoke very clear and educated Russian so clearly was not a peasant nor anything like one. The traditional costume she was wearing was simply for the job in hand: making a living or at least a bit of one entertaining tourists with demonstrations of what peasant life was like in Tsarist times. Sub-text: "This is how the people living in these parts used to do things. We don't live like this now, but we can show you what it was like."

As we stood outside the farmhouse Galina asked: *"Does anyone want to use the toilet? It's a few yards up the garden through a gate."*

Some took the opportunity.

While the rest of us were waiting Galina asked, *"Does anyone speak Russian?"*

"Yes, I can speak a bit," I offered.

"Where are you from?"

"England. And you?"

"I come from over to the east. I came here when I got married."

Some houses had decorated shutters.

The village road leading to our reception.

Invited inside, the low door opened directly onto some stairs. We went up and across the landing into a room on the left, laid for a traditional peasant feast. First, a soup of meat and vegetables – but it wasn't *bookhler*, the traditional Buryat soup of mutton and potatoes which we'd enjoyed the previous night as our first course when having dinner in our hotel in Ulan Ude. We then had a glass of cranberry juice and another of what they told us was home-made wine but was in fact distilled and tasted rather like brandy. Slices of cold omul*, a small white fish indigenous to Lake Baikal and rather like herring. Then slices of pork fat, then a puff pastry version of bread along with ordinary bread, tomatoes and sweet cakes. Then some cream and honey which mix very well, and glasses of tea.

I slipped outside to wash my hands and caught Galina in animated conversation on her mobile phone. Even in the back of nowhere in Buryatia the locals were up to date with modern technology! Technologically, Galina was ahead of me – I don't possess a mobile phone.

After lunch, the four ladies conducted us to the barn, where they sang a religious song, then a cheerful song of welcome and then said they wanted to show us how weddings were conducted in the old days. Mike was grabbed and dressed in a yellow rubashka* (a Russian peasant shirt) and a cloth cap with a yellow plastic sunflower on the peak. One of the London ladies was decked out in bridal costume to the accompaniment of an appropriate folk song. It was all good fun until Ala disappeared to consult the other guide and our driver while the demonstration was going on, leaving me desperately trying to translate. Clearly in tsarist times a village wedding was a big occasion and everyone took part.

Our next port of call was on a group of Old Believers, who lived in the village of Tarbagatai*. Our host was a young man named Alexander, who showed us what he called his museum. It was full to bursting point with old household utensils such as saucepans, flatirons, beds, photos, posters, old farm implements and ploughs, horse-drawn carriages and even some very old books.

But most of the objects were covered in dust or just simply dirty and were not laid out in any particular order. There were very few labels and the ones I could see were almost indecipherable because they were written using the 'old orthography', the form of Cyrillic script used before the Revolution. An early reform was to modernise the style of writing, simplify spelling and virtually abolish some letters of the alphabet as unnecessary encumbrances. If you've ever tried to read a parish register written in Tudor times, you'll know what I mean about 'old fashioned' handwriting! Moreover, in many cases the ink had faded with age. To my mind this was less a museum, more a junk yard with a roof on.

The guests are greeted with a song of welcome.

Across the road was their newly restored cathedral. It was tiny, the icons inside looked just the same to us as those in Orthodox churches, and even though there was only room for a couple of dozen worshippers they had a small souvenir stall set up in a corner rather than in the entrance lobby as one might expect.

When we pressed Ala to explain to us what it is that distinguishes Old Believers from the rest of the Orthodox communion and why they have their own Patriarch in Moscow she struggled. This was hardly surprising when she herself was a Buddhist and not a follower of Orthodoxy, either Old or New. It appeared that in the 1650s the Patriarch Nikon introduced a number of reforms in the liturgy and practices of the Russian Orthodox Church, for example how many fingers you should use when crossing yourself, the correct order for the pieces of music in a sung service and what style of singing. This raised a fundamental question: should the Russian Church stick to its own traditions or accept the practices of the Greek Orthodox, which is where it originated from back in the ninth century?

Some clergy and worshippers refused to accept any of these reforms, and

The Old Believers' Cathedral in Tarbagatai

were nicknamed Old Believers. They stuck to their beliefs through centuries of persecution and still persist, for example, in adhering to the pre-Reform practice of crossing themselves with two fingers and not three – representing God the Father and God the Son but not including God the Holy Spirit. There are a number of other differences in ritual which seem comparatively minor to a non-Orthodox, who can't understand why it matters so much. I suppose if you believe in something that's all that matters – belief. Whether or not it makes any sense is not a consideration.

Farther north and west the scenery is what most people associate with Siberia: endless steppe or endless pine or birch forest, as Mike and I had observed from the window of our compartment on the railway during our journey from Moscow to Irkutsk – four days if you don't get off at any intervening stations. Here in southern Siberia the countryside is extremely attractive, and nothing like the popular image. It is well-wooded, and here was cut through by the Selenga*, a major river with broad meanders because the terrain is more or less flat. The river rises in Mongolia and many others flow into it before it falls into Lake Baikal. Its delta extends over an area of 680km^2 and is an important wetland nature reserve.

The contemplation of this bucolic scene prompts me to think that this may be an appropriate moment to draw this story to an end and take my leave.

September 2012

[Adapted from 'Jottings from the Trans-Siberian Railway'. Other books are listed inside the front cover.]

Guide to Pronunciation in Russian

Ala:	**Eh**-*la*
Buryat:	**Boo**-*ree-yat*
Desyatnikovo:	*Dess-**yat**-nee-kuh-vuh*
Ivolginsk:	*Ee-vol-**ghinsk***
omul:	**omm**-*ull*
rubashka:	*roo-**bash**-ka*
Tarbagatai:	*Tar-bag-a-**tie***
Ulan Ude:	*Oo-**lahn** Oo-**deh***
Selanga:	*Se-lan-**ga***

Postscript

In a tree in a wood outside a village deep in rural Russia a bird had built its nest and hatched out its chicks. One of them fell out and landed on a path below, where it chirped loudly, calling for its mother to rescue it. Which, of course, the mother bird couldn't do.

Along came Sergey, a peasant boy, on his way to the fields to feed the cattle. He heard the chick, picked it up and stuffed it inside his rubashka to keep it warm while he looked for somewhere safe to leave it for its mother to find it.

When he reached the field where the cattle were grazing, he saw a pile of fresh cow dung. He took the chick out from under his shirt and popped it in the warm dung for safety until its mother found it, and went on his way.

Slowly the chick began to sink into the dung and started to cheep frantically before it drowned.

A passing fox heard the chick's cries, pulled it out and then swallowed it whole.

The moral of this story is:

1. If someone drops you in it, they don't necessarily mean you any harm;
2. If someone pulls you out of it, they don't necessarily mean you any good;
3. And if you're in it – keep your bloody mouth shut.
   Goodnight

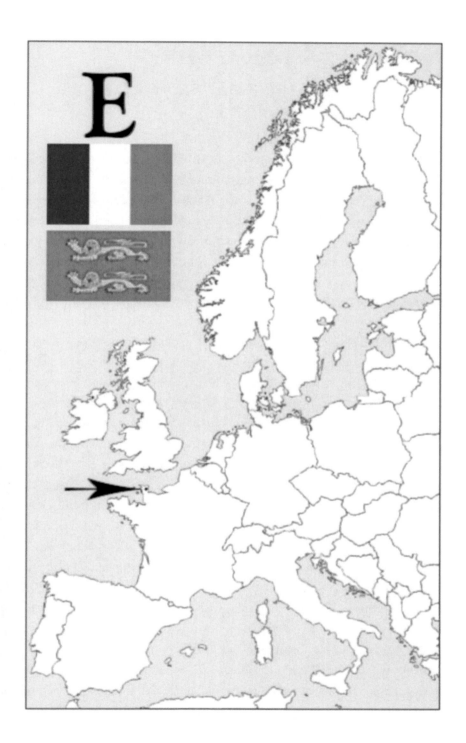

Ste-Mère Église
...And the Band Played On

As a result of regular trips via Cherbourg to Brittany and farther south Margaret and I had worked out a plan for the return journey. We'd spend our last night in one of our favourite towns, Dinan, at our favourite hotel, the Arvor, and make our way to the ferry at leisure allowing time to stop for some food somewhere. Through trial and error, we'd worked out that having found a pleasant restaurant with reliable parking at a suitable point, we could so arrange our timing as to be there around midday for lunch. One of our regular stopping places was at Coutances, a little to the west of where the Normandy landings took place in 1944.

The town itself is a fairly unremarkable little place, a centre for yachting and leisure sailing. Our chosen restaurant, the Neapolitaine, was down by the water, and had good parking across the road so the car was in full view from our table while we ate – a useful bonus. When you know you have to be at the ferry terminal by a certain hour and will need time for a bit of serious grocery shopping in the supermarket for specialities which you can't find in England, for example regional cheeses such as Livarot, which I'm particularly partial to, it takes the pressure off when you know exactly where your lunch stop is and can be confident that when you get there you'll be able to park the car in full view.

On one of our lunch stops things took an unexpected turn. We'd finished and were returning to the car when we heard music. It was a fine, sunny day and a band was playing somewhere close by. We went to investigate and discovered a large crowd of locals listening to an open-air concert by a French Army ensemble, playing popular melodies and with solos, duets, trios and quartets by individuals or sections of the band and, as often as not, not on their regular instruments. For example, bagpipes! But then bagpipes are a traditional Celtic instrument, and the province of Brittany has a Celtic tradition. It was not so surprising for the French army to feature the music and instruments of a part of the country many of its recruits come from.

What I remember so clearly was the relaxed atmosphere of the whole occasion. The concert was free, no one was hassling you to buy refreshments or souvenirs or a programme or jangling a collecting tin in front of you. It was simply local people enjoying a Sunday afternoon in the open air overlooking the harbour, listening to the performers and applauding enthusiastically. The soldiers and the bandmaster were obviously enjoying the occasion just as much and relishing the appreciation. The crowd contained all generations and it was as bucolic a scene as you could possibly want.

I think the Cotentin is much underrated as a tourist destination. We Brits tend to land at Cherbourg and straight away it's heads down and belt the length of the peninsula en route for our holiday destination, and don't think of looking at the attractions closer to hand. Margaret and I spent a lot of odd days exploring when we were a bit ahead of schedule before joining the queue at the ferry terminal and were rewarded with some interesting afternoons.

One day we found a signpost pointing to a château, and ended up at Pirou. Where? I've never yet met anyone who's even heard of it, let alone been there. It's halfway down the peninsula on the right-hand side, or halfway up on the left if you're on your way home. In plain English, it's on the west coast. The château is accessed via a complicated gateway which leads to a fortified farmhouse. As the *gardien* explained to me as we bought our tickets to gain entry, it had only recently been discovered by pure chance when, during building works, some doorways were altered and some wall facings and plaster were removed. The old house (it's hardly a 'château' – it's not big enough) is not a place I'd beg you to drive a hundred miles to see, but when you're on your way back to the ferry and have a couple of hours in hand it's well worth the minor detour.

We rounded off our pit-stop by finding a restaurant for lunch and squeezing in amongst the locals. It was a Sunday and they were all there *en famille*. We were interested to read the timetable for the seasonal ferry to Jersey which runs from the little harbour in summer.

On another drive to catch the ferry we thought we'd stop for lunch at Ste-Mère-Eglise. Uh, uh. Road jam-packed with army vehicles and blokes in WW2 uniforms. What's going on? Thought the war was over!

It was the weekend prior to 6 June and approaching the fiftieth anniversary of the Normandy landings. The village was *en fête* celebrating the part it had played, in particular a celebrated incident where an American paratrooper, by name John Steele, who when he dropped to earth, snagged his parachute on the spire of the church and was forced to dangle there helplessly throughout a two-hour battle unable either to take part or get out of the firing line. Captured by the

Germans, he soon escaped and within only a few hours had re-joined his colleagues when they attacked the town again. He survived that battle, and made regular visits back to the scene of his fame until he died in old age in the 1990s.

Behind the Gatehouse, Pirou.

We were lucky to find somewhere to park. It was quite odd to meet up with a group of chaps in US Army uniform sitting in a jeep and on overhearing a bit of their chat, discover that they were speaking Dutch! The uniform being worn was no indication whatsoever of the nationality of the wearer. You'd see a couple of GIs, say something to them in English and they'd turn out to be Germans sporting the costume of the erstwhile enemy.

It's all to do with dressing up and pretending – and by the way, that's not a criticism. We have our re-enactment societies back in Britain who go around dressed as Roman legionaries and demonstrate Roman infantry drill, or others who re-enact Civil War battles for the amusement of paying visitors and presumably to the exasperation of their long-suffering wives and girl-friends – who end up *faute de mieux* as camp followers doing the cooking and the laundry.

Many years ago, I watched a re-enactment of the Battle of Cheriton – a Civil War skirmish which took place in 1644. What I found peculiarly incongruous was one particular chap in full Cavalier costume who was rushing up and down just inside the fence shouting orders at his troops, but still wearing horn-rimmed glasses and with a camera dangling from his neck. Realistic – not. But I digress.

The main town of the Cotentin is, of course, the working harbour of Cherbourg. It's not itself a tourist resort, but the gateway to France for hundreds of thousands of British travellers getting on or off the ferry. Aware that many of those coming to France on holiday or just finishing such a visit will pass through their town, sensible entrepreneurs have ensured that there are rows of cafés and good quality restaurants located cheek by jowl alongside the harbour and around the main square. They know they have a captive market, or rather, two captive markets, depending on which direction the visitors are heading, and can rely on having plenty of customers.

For many years we were regular patrons of La Renaissance, a small hotel just off the town centre, near enough to enable us – once we'd found a parking space (not always easy!) – to walk to the restaurant area or possibly seek out one of our favourites, the Café du Théâtre on the market square, where we were particularly seduced by the comfortable seating and the menu's nice line in escargots.

Another time we drove along the coast eastwards to Barfleur, in the north-east corner of the peninsula, famous as William the Conqueror's point of departure when he set sail for England in 1066 to challenge King Harold for the throne. From there it's only a dozen miles down the coast to St Vaast-la-Hougue, renowned for its oysters – a claim for which I can personally vouch.

But what with bands playing unannounced, Germans dressed as GIs, dummies of paratroopers hanging off church spires or scouring the line-up of harbour side restaurants in Cherbourg trying to decide who's offering the best deal on an assiette de fruits de mer – you never know what you'll find next in the Cotentin and may even be spoilt for choice.

June 1993

Postscript

Prostitutes in Portsmouth try to attract custom from visiting French sailors on shore leave by reciting the motto of the French Navy: 'At sea, it's time'. Or, in French: '*A l'eau, c'est l'heure*'.

Goodnight.

Entering Pirou through the Gatehouse.

SOUTHAMPTON

Freemantle
La Vie de Bohème!

At Southampton in the 1950s the holder of an open university scholarship, or 'scholar', as well as half board and all tuition fees paid was entitled to accommodation for all three undergraduate years in a hall of residence. It was quite a bonus not having to find digs and live under the eye of some Mrs Buggins who might not approve of student ways.

But once I'd graduated and embarked on a PGCE (Post-Graduate Certificate in Education), it was up to me to find for myself somewhere to live. As luck would have it, my friend John Wallbridge who had been in many ways my mentor during my student days and as chairman of Op Soc had got me involved in student productions of Gilbert & Sullivan, owned a 'semi' in Heysham Road in Freemantle, a down-at-heel late Victorian inner suburb of Southampton. He offered it to me as the official tenant with responsibility for the three other young men I would need to share with to help pay the rent. And he said, archly, "I'm not having you fathering children on my springs!" Point taken.

My obvious first choice of co-habitee was Mike, in his final year, who features in other stories. A second was Jim, in appearance no oil painting and wearing thick glasses and taking finals in German, who to no one's surprise went on to get a First. Then Peter, a fresher reading French whom I'd met at Op Soc rehearsals and who became a life-long friend. However, university regulations insisted that first year students lived either in Hall or digs. When the authorities found out he was living unsupervised in a house he got moved out fairly quickly much against his – and our – wishes. He was replaced by another Peter, and when he left, by John.

In such a small house, it wasn't feasible to live independently of each other, so we quickly worked out how we'd run the establishment. We each had a bedroom, but would share the front room for recreation, reading, entertaining and generally lounging about and smoking. No, we didn't have a telly.

The dining room would be just that and we would have a proper dinner every night and take turns in preparing the meal. The kitchen had a door opening onto a small back garden where I kept my motor bike, a Royal Enfield 350cc. At the

48

end of the garden was a four-foot high chain-link fence with a gate onto a gravel road and the front gardens of the row of houses behind us – i.e. their front rooms looked into our back garden and the back of our house. Behind those houses was Shirley High St. All the necessary shops were there, and on a Sunday morning I would wander into the newsagent in my pyjamas, dressing gown and slippers and buy my copy of The Observer without anyone turning a hair. We even had a cinema on the corner, where I remember seeing a wonderful Tosca with Renata Tebaldi doing the singing and Sophia Loren doing the panting. And Tito Gobbi as a most dramatic, evil Scarpia – wow!

We put a list on the wall with our four names across the top, repeated in columns downwards. When you'd cooked dinner, you crossed your name off. Whoever was highest on the list was duty cook for the next day, unless he had some overriding reason for not doing so, e.g. a lecture, the deadline for an essay or a date. But if you missed your turn and the others crossed their names off, their names dropped down the lists while yours remained where it was floating ever higher until there came a point where you might be three or four dinner duties in arrears and would find yourself cooking for several successive days in order to get down the list and on level terms again with the rest of the household.

Other rules applied to dinner: you had to serve a main course and a dessert of some kind and were not allowed to use anything straight out of a tin, e.g. baked beans. At least one fresh vegetable in addition to the customary staple – the humble spud. This was, of course, long before the days of freezers, though we did have a small fridge. Chinese restaurants and the panorama of ethnic cuisines which are nowadays to be found in every suburb and even many villages were unheard of – in those days there was no such thing as 'a takeaway'. The only food available to the public was in a proper restaurant (far too expensive for us) or a portion of fish and chips from the 'chippy', wrapped in newspaper and eaten in the street walking home. Pubs only offered bread and cheese, pickled onions, scotch eggs and packets of crisps. Microwaves had yet to be invented.

To encourage imaginative cooking, we also decreed that whoever cooked didn't do his own washing up. He left it for whoever was 'on' next day. He was free to choose whether to do it after dinner and stack it to dry for the morrow, or leave it and wash it all up while cooking the meal.

Individually we worked out a range of dishes which we'd specialise in, and I asked my mother to teach me how to roast half a pig's head, bake an eel in a casserole and how to make pastry so that I could make my own Cornish pasties.

I already knew how to make custard either thick or thin according to what it was to go with and I frequented the local fruiterer to see what was on offer or in season to make my dessert – often making a fruit pie rather than just stewing the fruit or serving it raw. My colleagues did the same and we had a decent dinner every night and a wide range of dishes according to who was serving it up. It may sound a bit regimented, but it worked, we ate healthily and each honed his culinary skills.

After dinner, percolated coffee was served in the lounge and Mike and I smoked our pipes. At weekends, we often invited our girlfriends to join us for dinner and as I'd been in the Navy during national service and was accustomed to the hard stuff served in the wardroom I took it upon myself to educate my younger colleagues by laying in a range of liqueurs and teaching them how to enjoy them. Into the bargain, the girls were most impressed by our sophistication. (*Smirk!*)

This leads me on to a reminiscence of a different order. Attending the United Nations Student Association (UNSA) conference in Durham I met a girl from those parts who, despite wearing very thick glasses, I thought quite pretty and interesting and she obviously took a bit of a shine to me. We exchanged addresses and wrote to each other. Taking advantage of having a spare bed in the interim between Peter leaving and John arriving I invited her to pay me a visit – bringing a friend with her to guarantee her personal safety in a house full of young men – if you follow. The two girls came. We laid on food and good company and made them welcome. I thought Cindy would wonder what was wrong if I didn't at least kiss her goodnight, but when I put my arms around her waist and attempted to do so, as far as I leaned forward she leaned back just out of reach and continued to lean farther than I thought backs could go except for contortionists. If I hadn't let go we'd have both fallen over. I have never managed to make sense of it. She'd paid a rail fare to travel all the way from Yorkshire to see me – yet rebuffed even a goodnight kiss! When we parted at the railway station, it wasn't 'au revoir', Cynthia, but 'Adieu'!

Cooking seriously for the first time, inevitably we all had mishaps. The first time I made Cornish pasties I got the quantities wrong and through the glass front of the oven watched in horror as they expanded and expanded and looked likely to burst the door open! Luckily the proportions of pastry to filling were correct so they tasted fine – just twice the size per person to what I'd intended. Had to make a lot more gravy at the double!

Then there was the time John, our new arrival, had riled us just once too often by displaying yet again that he didn't really have a sense of humour (his German girlfriend was similarly devoid). Mike and I decided to have a bit of fun at his expense. I was serving pig's head, which I usually carved in the kitchen and brought in on the plates. This time I just cut off the end of the snout, got Mike to

distract John and while he was turning to his left to talk to Mike, I served from the right and put down his plate with just the snout on it with the nostrils pointing upwards. John turned back, saw two nostrils in the middle of his otherwise empty plate looking up at him and nearly had a fit! Of course, once we'd stopped laughing, we took it away and gave him a proper portion of roast pork. But we'd made our point. Lighten up, John, for God's sake.

Then there was the time Mike and I decided it was time we 'goosed' Jim, who didn't have that sort of sense of humour. We waited until he was bending forward to take the meat out of the oven and had both his hands in the oven glove, then each of us in turn ran a hand up his protruding bottom. Jim's cries of strident objection to being defiled while unable to defend his honour due to holding a hot roasting dish with both hands remain a cherished memory to this day.

Then there was the mouse. We heard scratching noises in our store cupboard and opened it to investigate. The mouse had hidden behind a jam jar but had given himself away by leaving his tail sticking out. I put my finger on it, moved the jar, held him up by his tail, he doubled back on it and bit me, I yelped, dropped him and he scarpered. One, nil. Next time I was prepared. I had an empty jam jar ready. I grabbed the mouse's tail and swung him around and around by it so that he couldn't double up, dropped him in the jar and put the lid on. Gotcha!

"Now, where's Trousers?"

'Trousers' was next door's soppy ha'porth of a cat, who had very fluffy hind legs – hence our nickname for him – and who loved to lie on his back and have his tummy tickled. I showed Trousers the mouse standing up inside the jam jar desperately trying to find a way out and Trousers seemed less than interested – probably overfed by his owner and never had to catch his own dinner in his life. But we thought that if we let the mouse out of the jar nature would take over and he'd pounce on it. Mike held him by his hind quarters while I put the jam jar sideways on the floor and unscrewed the lid – expecting the mouse to run out, be swatted with a large paw and carried off into the garden to meet his fate. Not a bit of it. The mouse shot out straight between Trousers' front paws, under his body, under his hind legs and straight out the door. Trousers, taken completely by surprise, tried to turn himself inside out left and right all at the same time and ended up in a heap on the floor. So did we! Talk about laugh! Mouse – one. Nimrod, Mighty Hunter – nil.

Despite being now rather removed from the university campus, I still maintained some involvement. I'd always taken part in Rag Week, one year editing the Rag magazine, Goblio, and doing a conjuring act in the Rag Show, in another taking part in an Edwardian Music Hall. This year I dressed up as a tramp, donned my roller skates and with two friends wove my way through the main department stores to the general consternation of the shoppers who nonetheless gave generously when we held out our collection tins for the Rag charities. I then led a procession up Above Bar (the main shopping street in Southampton city centre) and finally, there being no buses to take me back home, got my friend Alan Young to give me a tow.

I was still involved in the University Operatic Society, in the chorus in *The Sorcerer*, one of Gilbert & Sullivan's lesser-known operas, and as Cox in *Cox and Box*, the one-act musical farce Sullivan composed with the librettist F. C. Burnand. However, fed up with fellow students dismissing our endeavours as 'You can only sing G & S, you can't sing 'real' opera', we decided to show them that indeed we could, albeit sometimes not in the same key as a professional. In a concert imaginatively entitled 'Pick of the Ops'(!) we performed excerpts from grand opera as solos, duets or ensemble. Peter (bass) sang 'Myself when young' from Liza Lehmann's song-cycle 'In a Persian garden' based on the Rubaiyat of Omar Khayyam. The high point for me was joining our leading soprano, Hilary Taylor, to sing Rodolfo and Mimi falling in love at the end of Act 1 of *La Bohème* – hence the sub-title of this chapter! We heard no more accusations that 'you can only sing G & S'! And incidentally: why 'only'? G & S is quite demanding, as anyone will acknowledge who's sat through an amateur performance where the second-tier soloists aren't really up to it…

The notice says 'Save petrol!' As a result of the Suez
Crisis, it was rationed at the time.

Otherwise, I turned out when required for the cricket 2nd XI, and although I didn't play rugby, I was welcome in the bar for the club's post-match sing-song because of my extensive repertoire of rude limericks and other 'dirty ditties' from my time in the navy.

There was an old lady living in the house directly behind us who clearly disapproved of students and their goings on and if she was at her front door when one of us went out of our back gate to go shopping would pointedly ignore us even if we said 'Good morning'. If we had a party over a weekend, she used to watch us from behind her lace curtains, thinking we didn't know she was there. The phrase 'Silly Old Bag' came to mind. We weren't doing anything wrong, such as getting drunk or making excessive noise and we objected to her clandestine surveillance and self-appointed disapproval. How to sort her out, once and for all? One Sunday morning we all lined up with our lady guests outside the back door in various states of semi-undress and waved to her, knowing she was lurking behind her curtain. As soon as she realised that we were waving to her she let the curtain go and it hung straight – we all cheered and gave her a round of applause.

Despite our having lived together for several months in a fairly confined space, three of my house-mates I never saw again. But some student friendships last for life.

I had by this time acquired a 'serious' girlfriend who later admitted that what first drew her to me was that I had a beard. Nigh impossible as it may be for a modern reader to comprehend, living today in a world where every Tom, Dick or Harry in any job or profession can freely choose whether to shave or not and if so, how often, in the 1950s sporting a full set of whiskers was so unusual that passers-by would turn their heads and gaze in disbelief and others, unprompted, would proffer knowing assertions that you must be trying to hide something.

As the attraction was returned, I will leave to your imagination what two fit and healthy young people aged twenty and twenty-five respectively got up to while savouring the pleasures of a horizontal cuddle in what she referred to as 'enjoying my amenities' while, for her part, equally enjoying mine. Only don't blame me if you have that sort of an imagination.

Margaret, the 'serious girlfriend', and I got married. Mike was best man and Peter (of Op Soc fame) was an usher. Both joined us for a reception and photograph in the Mayor's Parlour when Margaret was Mayor of Eastleigh for the first time and by happenstance this coincided with our silver wedding anniversary. They joined us again for lunch at a well-known local hostelry when we marked our golden wedding.

The following year both were with me at her humanist civic funeral, the coffin borne into the crematorium draped with the borough flag and coat of arms and topped by her OBE insignia and her four civic medals as a past mayor (twice), a past mayoress and a Freeman of the Borough. Peter delivered one of the eulogies, followed by Kevin Price JP, a former colleague from the Southampton Bench where she was a magistrate for thirty years and finally by Keith House, the Leader of the Council, where Margaret sat, also for thirty years, after being elected as the first-ever Liberal member and where later she became the first Liberal to be Leader of the Council.

In the Mayor's Parlour in Eastleigh. Peter and Mike are on the far left.

All because our lives became inextricably entangled in our student days in that house of somewhat decorous ill-fame in Freemantle.

October 1957 – July 1958

Postscript

Doctor:	"Yes, Mrs Brown, what can I do for you?"
Mrs Brown:	"It's not me, it's about my husband."
Doctor:	"What about him?"
Mrs Brown:	"He keeps blowing smoke rings."
Doctor:	"What's wrong with that?"
Mrs Brown:	"He doesn't smoke."

Goodnight.

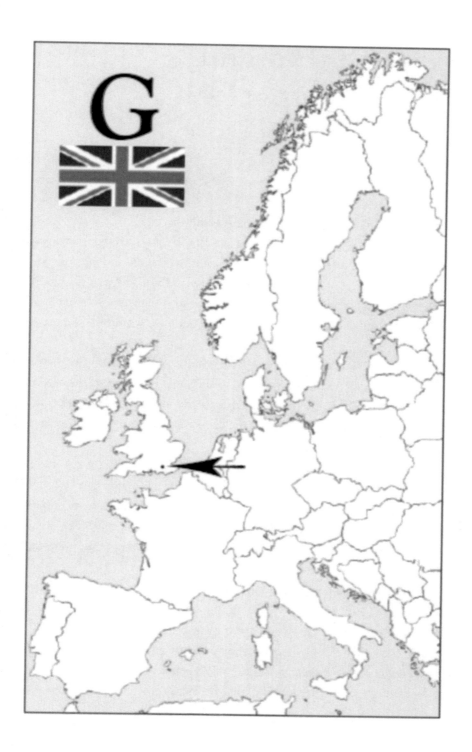

G

Gatwick
'S No Joke!

It's highly likely that you, dear reader, will have been through Gatwick Airport. I very much hope that your experience was nothing like mine in the spring of 2018.

An unseasonal cold burst was forecast to hit the UK on 1 March – sub-zero air from Siberia which the media christened 'the Beast from the East'. It would bring heavy snow across the whole country and would cause major disruptions of road, rail and air traffic. Everyone was advised not to travel unless it was absolutely essential, and in some parts of the country, such as across the Pennines or on high ground farther north, not at all. They just wouldn't be able to get through.

At that time, I had a timeshare in Lanzarote in the Canaries. I had arranged to stay for a fortnight and was scheduled to fly home on – you've guessed it! – 1 March. Of course, I'd made the arrangements months before. No one – least of all me – was expecting a white-out on the day I was scheduled to return. Buggers luck, as they say.

'The Beast from the East' arrived as expected, and I flew straight into it.

Actually, not straight. My flight was delayed for three hours. Why? Snow on the runway in Arrecife? No, of course not. It was because several airports in Britain, notably Glasgow, Edinburgh and East Midlands, had been forced to close because of the weather, which meant that flights were being diverted and planes were not in the right place when required.

I was sitting in the departure lounge at Arrecife with a passenger whose UK airport was shut and who was expecting an announcement shortly about those passengers having to spend the night in the airport, sleeping rough.

"They knew this was happening when we were still in our hotel. Why didn't our travel agent tell us then?" she asked. "We could have booked in for another night. Instead of that, we're going to be stuck here for twenty-four hours."

I sympathised.

My friend Carol of some forty years standing who runs a stables where I used to have my council seat, had spent the second week with me in Lanzarote but was returning on an earlier flight. Our arrangement was that she would wait for me at luggage check-out at Gatwick and her daughter, Verity, would collect us both and drive us home.

I arrived three hours behind schedule, at 22h30. Carol was waiting. The airport was shutting down for the night.

"Do you want the bad news first, or the bad news?" she asked. "Verity can't get the van up the slope over the motorway bridge because of ice and in any case the M3 is blocked by jack-knifed vehicles. She can't get here. There are no hotel rooms to be had. We're stuck for the night. On top of that, my mobile's cracking up as it's running out of charge."

Things got worse. There were no trains running, so we couldn't even get to London and try our luck getting a train home. As it happened, we saw on the TV news the following day that the train we might well have caught got stuck in the New Forest between Ringwood and Christchurch when the power failed and the unfortunate passengers spent sixteen hours marooned without heat, light or food. The TV news showed some of them sleeping on the luggage racks!

Here at Gatwick, no one appeared to be in charge. We wandered back to the all-night café, bagged an armchair each and resigned ourselves to a long and uncomfortable night, leaning back for neck and head support and resting our feet on our luggage. The lights would be on all night, but at least between fitful snoozes we would be able to get a cup of coffee or a slice of cake and take it in turn to go to the loo. The waiting staff, young and from various parts of the continent, were friendly and helpful but they weren't in a position to offer advice about accommodation, emergency services if required or rail or bus availability. In any case, it wasn't their job. They were simply baristas.

I wandered off to the gents at about midnight, noting that all available upright chairs had been taken and people were trying to sleep in all sorts of uncomfortable poses. Those without even a chair were sitting or lying on the bare tiled floor, some awake, others with their hats or hoods pulled over their eyes, curled up in the foetal position with their luggage behind their knees sleeping as best they could.

Again, the absence of any officials on duty was glaring. What would happen if someone was taken ill? A pregnant woman started to give birth? A child went missing? A fight broke out? Someone got drunk? Some lone passenger went to the loo and on his return found his luggage had been interfered with and, say, his laptop stolen? I just couldn't understand how a major airport could be so remiss, bearing in mind that passengers having to spend the night would be an everyday (or every night) occurrence whenever they missed their connection.

A couple of hours later I went off to the gents for a second time. What befell me there is not for the squeamish and is printed in italics at the end of this story. It explains in even greater detail why my night in Gatwick is forever etched in my memory. If you don't have a strong stomach, don't read it. If, against my advice, you do decide to read it, be prepared for it being forever etched in yours.

Back in the café, Carol was blearily awake. I muttered something about 'coffee' and we took it in turns to queue up. She didn't appear to notice that I was wearing my white lightweight summer trousers in place of my normal green ones. I deemed it prudent to let sleeping dogs lie and not to draw attention to my change of attire.

Shortly after 5 a.m. we awoke fitfully, to see three very large policemen carrying weapons wandering through the café. We presumed that they'd been here all night, or were changing shift. What was certain was that they had not been patrolling during the night, but had been closeted away somewhere ready for any emergency.

In the meantime, Carol was frantically trying to contact Verity and failing each time to get through. We went downstairs, to see if we could get a coach to London or, frankly, to anywhere.

"The company's run from Bournemouth," said the booking clerk in the coach company's office, shamefacedly. "The staff can't get in, so the head office is closed. I don't know if we have any coaches running or if they are, then where they're running to."

"No coaches," I said to Carol. "There's nothing else for it, we'll have to try the trains."

At that moment, Carol's mobile rang. As she took the call, her face lit up with relief. It was Verity on the phone.

"She says she's been trying all morning to get hold of me, but I'm always engaged. That's because whenever I've been trying to ring her, she's been trying to ring me! She says she left home at six this morning and she's here in the car park! I've told her where we are and she's coming to find us."

A few minutes later, Verity showed up. It was some distance through the parking bays to where she'd parked the van, but worth every step! My summer trousers complied with the laws of decency but were woefully inadequate for the sub-zero temperature at nine in the morning. I climbed into the back seat and found that I'd have a dog as a travelling companion.

"She gets upset if I drive anywhere without her," explained Verity. "She'll go to sleep the moment I drive off."

And so, it turned out. I passed most of the journey with a damp muzzle resting in my lap. We drove home unhindered as the snow had been cleared from the main roads. I was deposited at my front door with my luggage twelve hours late – and what a twelve hours! But otherwise none the worse for wear that a shower and some clean clothes wouldn't put right. Although the memory of that night will fade it will never disappear. I hope never again to arrive at an airport after it's effectively shut down for the night – snow or not.

1 March 2018

Postscript

An amorous pheasant fancied a lady partridge, so he sidled up to her and whispered, "Are you game?"

Goodnight

The rest of this story is not recommended reading for the squeamish, who for safety's sake should pass over the next five pages without looking and turn directly to page 67. Be warned!

It was between one and two in the morning and I was standing at the urinal in the gents passing water when I was aware of a sudden movement in my bowels and a distinct 'plop'. "Good God," I thought, "I've filled my pants!" And I had – I could feel the weight. But before I could move to the next thought phase – what to do, how to remove my underpants without messing up my trousers, how to empty them out, how to rinse them and get back to my luggage in the café and retrieve a clean pair from my case, any ideas I had of disaster management were trumped.

Without any warning, my bowels emptied as though a cork had been taken off a champagne bottle. They simply exploded. My underpants being already full, the rest of the movement shot directly down my right trouser leg as far as the ankle. I couldn't believe it! Here I was, standing at a urinal alongside other users, and suddenly and without any warning I had hot excrement running down my leg in imminent danger of filling my shoes. It's not a situation anyone ever expects to happen to them in real life and so prepares for, there aren't any courses teaching you how to deal with such a contingency, you're caught completely off guard and there's no time to plan your response and on top of that you're in a public space. You have to think on your feet and take immediate action.

Behind me were the cubicles, and I shot into the end one and closed the door. Gingerly, I slid my trousers down, then my pants, and crouched over the pedestal. Tearing paper off the adjacent roll, I proceeded to clean my person so that it was safe to sit down, then as my trousers were now on the floor to clean as much as I could a handful at a time, dropping the soiled paper into the lavatory pan behind me. Eventually I succeeded in removing most of the solid and realised that as it was only half-digested it was the remnants of the meal I'd eaten on the flight. Once the solid matter was removed it was safe to try to wriggle my feet out of my trousers and then out of my pants and fold them over. I intended to empty them directly into the lavatory bowl and then rinse them in the sink outside.

Having cleaned up my trousers as much as possible I had, of course, no option but to put them back on. How else was I going to get back to the café and put on my spare pair? I could hardly wander through the airport concourse naked from the waist down.

It wasn't a pleasant experience walking all the way back to the café wearing soaking trousers, but I had no option. Rummaging through my case, I extracted my summer-weight white trousers. Fortunately, Carol was asleep, so was not a witness. When I reached the gents, a sign indicated that they were closed for cleaning. I peeped inside and found the man in charge, who told me that the disabled toilet was still available, just around the corner. There I had the place to myself and could change trousers and roll the soiled ones up and put them in a plastic carrier bag.

I then discovered that I'd mislaid my underpants. In the rush to rinse them, I'd wrung them out but then left them in the bowl!

I went back to the gents, pushed past the sign saying 'Closed for cleaning' and spotted them on the floor under a sink. The foreign women doing the cleaning looked on totally bemused as I pointed to them, bent down and snatched them up and fled the scene before anyone started asking questions. I reached the safe haven of the all-night café without anyone being any the wiser as to the traumatic experience I had just gone through.

Goodnight, again

NB Readers familiar with standard Anglo-Saxon terminology are welcome to read the above again, inserting the Anglo-Saxon words they might have used themselves had such an accident happened to them and they were telling their friends all about it. But this is, after all, a book for family consumption. The words I actually used in my head when experiencing this event, I leave to your imagination. And you will, I'm sure, agree that they're not fit to print.

Harlingen
On the Far Horizon

I first met Danny when she was only a toddler and her grandfather, my Dutch pen-friend, plonked her on my lap when I was an 18-year-old signalman serving in the RNVR (Royal Naval Volunteer Reserve) and my ship had docked in Amsterdam for a couple of days' shore leave. Since then, she often joined Margaret and I on holiday and since Margaret's death we've made a number of visits together around the Netherlands.

To reach the ferry at Harlingen she opted to take the train from Amsterdam as far as Alkmaar*, then the bus over the Afsluitdijk*, the twenty-mile-long embankment which carries a major causeway and was completed in 1932 to separate the Zuyder Zee* from the North Sea, with a lock at the northern end. There we had to change buses and get to Harlingen for the ferry to our destination, Terschelling*. This is the middle one of the Frisian Islands which run like a ribbon off the North Sea coast of the Netherlands and Germany up to the border with Denmark.

Lunch beside the canal in Harlingen.

Harlingen* is a very old town and the historic centre has some canals and seventeenth century houses. We arrived on time only to find that due to technical problems the midday ferry had been cancelled and we'd have to wait until midafternoon. Chance for a pleasant lunch. We sat watching the pleasure yachts and sailing boats making their way through the canal to the harbour, ready for some serious sailing on the Waddensee*, the stretch of water separating mainland Holland from the islands. To be technically accurate, we were no longer in Holland – a province of the Netherlands – but in Friesland*, a different province. They even speak their own language here – Fries*.

Terschelling and its neighbouring island Vlieland* are both visible on the horizon – only just, as they're pretty flat – but despite the lack of distance measured in miles or kilometres the ferry takes two hours. This is because you don't go in a straight line but have to zigzag following the channels to avoid going aground on the sandbanks which at low water are exposed. Despite appearing so benign on a sunny day with little wind the Waddensee is, in truth, a treacherous stretch of water. If you don't know your charts and are not skilled at handling your boat disaster is only a few feet away – left, right or underneath. The channels, although deep enough, are narrow and sinuous and there are buoys in a variety of shapes and colours dotted all over the place. The slightest deviation and you'll run aground.

Boarding the ferry to Terschelling.

The main settlement on the island is West Terschelling. The most obvious unusual feature of the town is that the main square is not dominated by the customary town hall or main church (or both) but by a lighthouse. Not, moreover, just any old lighthouse, but Brandaris*, a name famous throughout the Netherlands. The name is said to be derived from St Brendan, an Irish saint who in the fourth century, according to legend, spent seven years at sea trying without success to find the Promised Land. He is traditionally depicted carrying a flaming torch, hence his connection with lighthouses. He made landfall along the coasts of Brittany, where numerous villages owe their names to chapels erected in his honour during the Dark Ages. That he ever reached Terschelling is improbable, but perhaps the people putting up the original light thought naming it after the famous seafaring saint might bless their endeavours.

The first document to mention a light on the island is dated 1323, which shows how important it was to have some sort of navigational aid for local fishermen and for merchant vessels trying to find a safe passage between Terschelling and Vlieland on their way south into the Zuyder Zee and eventually to Amsterdam.

The present lighthouse is just over 50m high and has been in situ since 1594, with many restorations and renovations. Despite becoming automatic in 1977 it is still manned as the elevated position enables the keeper to survey a large section of the waters around the coast of North Holland. The importance of this surveillance means the look-out mustn't be distracted by tourists or visitors and therefore the building is not open to the public.

The Frisian Islands are a popular destination in high season for families anxious to take advantage of the wonderful beaches, which on Terschelling cover the entire northern side of the island – a stretch of some 30km of uninterrupted sand up to 500m wide and backed by dunes which protect the southern side where the inhabitants live.

Brandaris.

The wind was blowing strongly, so we decided not to hire bikes. Instead we took the bus to its terminus – Oosterend – as the eastern end of the island, where a huge nature reserve is located, is uninhabited and closed to motor vehicles but with some paths open to walkers and cyclists. We walked out to the top of the dyke protecting the southern coast, then back between fields with a few sheep and found a signboard depicting de Stins, a tall, narrow house built on an artificial mound and defended by a moat and drawbridge, traces of which had recently been discovered on the far side of the field. This discovery has confounded historians, who until then had been convinced that the islands had never been fortified.

By the time we regained the village it was midday and the village café was about to open. We enjoyed a restorative coffee, and time to savour the display around the walls of old advertising signs for all manner of household goods. Danny was highly amused as she could remember many of them from her childhood before they were superseded by modern brands.

The return bus wasn't due for an hour, so we decided to walk to the north coast, and got a nasty shock when we discovered how far that actually was. We reached the top of the dunes, only to find that they went on for another half mile or more before reaching the beach and then it looked as if it was as far again to the sea beyond.

"No way!" Danny recommended that we stop off for lunch at Midsland, a large village situated, as the name suggests, about halfway between one end of the island and the other. We chose a café called 'De Dammesaan', but when I asked Danny what that meant she said she didn't know. The waitress pointed to the café's sign: an earthenware pot enveloped in wickerwork, the way we – in England, too – used to protect liquids in transit. Farther along the road was a specialist cheese shop, where I took advice and bought a couple of Frisian specialities: very hard cheeses made with herbs and one with nettles. These would be something to amuse the folks back home.

The proliferation of ice cream parlours, coffee shops and displays of bunting showed the importance of tourism to the island's economy, but in fact fishing and farming are still important. The resident population is not far short of 5,000.

Back at our hotel the proprietor was embarrassed to have to ask us to move to another hotel for our third night as he'd taken our booking banking on some of his earlier reservations being cancelled and none of them had been! This was because of the weather forecast of fine sunny weather. Most of the visitors were older people like ourselves, enjoying an extended weekend break in a quiet location and without children around now that the schools had gone back.

Breakfast provided yet another peek into the regional cuisine of Friesland: sugar bread, a white loaf with small pieces of raw white sugar inserted (I can't imagine how it's done without caramelising it). Danny said no one makes it in Amsterdam anymore and you can only find it nowadays here in Friesland. Quite nice, though I probably wouldn't want it too often. It's very, very sweet, as you would expect and you slice it and spread butter on it just like ordinary bread. But I bought a loaf at the bakery to take home just to give friends a new gastronomic experience.

The wind was still blowing hard and there were frequent short, sharp showers, so it was a good excuse to visit the island's museum. There were exhibits showing the rooms of a typical house at the beginning of the last century, with costumed mannequins and all the usual household furniture. However, a whole section was given over to the exploits of the explorer Willem Barentsz, a native of Terschelling, who at the end of the sixteenth century was commissioned by Amsterdam merchants to go in search of a way around the top of Asia to enable Dutch merchant ships to reach the Far East.

At the time when Barentsz was trying to find the so-called 'North-East Passage' the famous English explorers Hudson, Davis and Frobisher were venturing into unknown waters around the top of Canada to try to find the better known 'North-West Passage' with the same purpose in mind: trade. On his first voyage Barentsz discovered Svalbard, which we know in English as Spitsbergen. Turning east, he explored the sea north of Norway and Russia which was subsequently named after him – the Barents Sea. As the winter of 1596 approached his ship was caught in the ice on the far side of Novaya Zemlya* and the crew had to build a wooden house in which to overwinter.

Barentsz himself and three other crew members didn't survive the ordeal, but when the ice melted in the spring the rest of those who had set sail for Russia were rescued and ultimately found their way back to Holland. The museum has a reconstruction of their house and pictures on the wall of the museum show the men fighting off hungry polar bears.

Many a woman lost a husband, brother or son in the treacherous waters of the Waddensee and a statue honouring their plight (dated 1993) has been erected on a high point overlooking the harbour depicting a woman in waterproofs gazing out to sea in the hope that her menfolk will return safely. From this point, it was fascinating to watch a succession of sailing ships leave harbour at studied intervals and all in 'line ahead' to all appearances like ducklings following the mother duck. They used their engines to proceed several hundred yards out to sea before reaching the buoy which marked the point where they had to turn sharply to port – demonstrating how absolutely vital it was that they kept to the channels marked by the buoys if they were not to run aground. There is very little room for a mistake, so it's clearly a good place for sailing enthusiasts and navigators to hone their skills.

September 2013

Guide to Pronunciation

Afsluitdijk:	*Aff-slout-dike*
Alkmaar:	*Al-uk-mar*
Brandaris:	*Bron-dar-iss*
Fries:	**Freece**
Friesland:	**Freece**-*lond*
Harlingen:	*Har-ling-uh*
Novaya Zemlya:	*Nov-igh-ya Z-yem-lyah*
Terschelling:	*Tair-skell-ing*
Vlieland:	*Vlee-lond*
Waddensee:	*Vudd-en-zay*
Zuyder Zee:	*Zowd-er Zay*

Postscript

Haberdashery Assistant:	"Good morning, sir. How can I help you?"
Customer:	"I'd like a box of a dozen handkerchiefs."
Haberdashery Assistant:	"Certainly, sir. What size nose?"

Goodnight

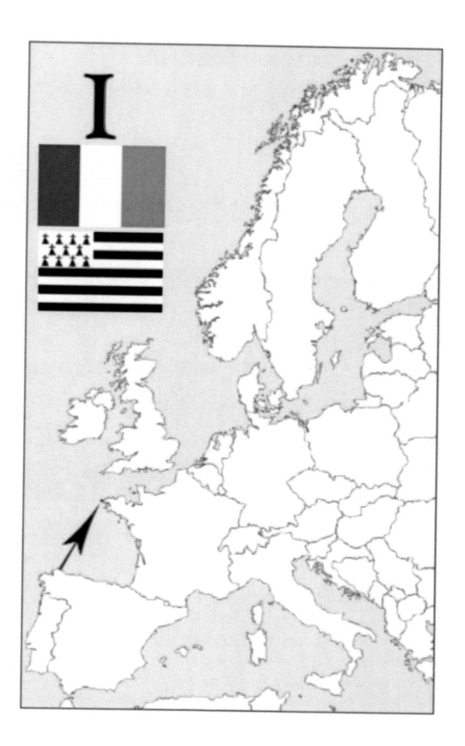

ÎLE de MOLÈNE
Making the Most of Nothing

[Conversations in italics were in French]

Even someone familiar with France and its islands may well admit to never having heard of Molène, and is even less likely to know where it is. It lies west of Brittany, midway between the mainland and its larger neighbour, Ouessant, better known by its English name: Ushant.

Most visitors arrive from Brest or the ferry port of Le Conquet, but we had decided to spend a few days on Ouessant first and go ashore at Molène on our way back.

I visited my first island off the French coast back in 1997 with my wife, Margaret, and two friends, and the experience gave me an idea: why not visit all the others? Over the course of the next dozen years Margaret and I enjoyed many holidays in France, and if we found ourselves near the coast and near an island we hadn't visited we'd book a trip: "Been there. Bought the tee-shirt (as a Christmas present for our elder son... of course). Drunk the coffee. Admired the view. Had the languorous lunch. Bought the fridge magnet." At the time of her death in 2011 we'd successfully ticked off about a third of the names on the atlas.

One of the lifestyle changes when you lose a partner is that holidays have to be arranged with new people. One needs some company, which takes time and mutual patience to organise. My opportunity arose in conversation with my friend Mike, who'd crossed Siberia with me five years before and taken the photos for the book we'd written together.

"You know about my project to visit all the islands off the French coast?"

"You may have mentioned it. Why do you ask?"

"Well, I haven't knocked any more off my list since Margaret died, and I feel it's time I got started again. The one I've got my eye on is Ushant, because it's the most distant and therefore the trickiest to get to. How about it? A few days enjoying French cuisine? You do the driving; I'll do the talking."

"How long do you propose? When we did Siberia, it took six weeks."

"Yes, but that was because we got side-tracked into crossing Mongolia as well. I'm only thinking of Ushant itself, and there's a little speck called Molène halfway between which we might as well visit *en passant*, so to speak. Ten days to a fortnight should do the trick, allowing for rest days to people-watch over a glass of something."

"I'll give it some thought."

When a few days later he came up with the right answer, I got cracking making hotel and ferry bookings while delegating to him responsibility for booking his car on the ferry to St Malo.

Most visitors to Molène arrive from the mainland – Brest or the ferry port of Le Conquet – but we, of course, were arriving from Ushant.

Entering the harbour, we had a fine view of the village and noted the road up from the jetty.

"Where's 'l'Archipel', please?" I asked the lady at Reception, referring to the hotel where we'd made a reservation.

"Oh – Monsieur Monot!" she remarked with satisfaction and delight. *"It's just up there, you'll see it. Just follow the path."*

"It seems," I muttered to Mike, "that this is such a small place that they don't have roads or signs because you always end up in the same place."

The concrete path gave way to tarmac, and as we cresting the rise and turned left, overlooking the village, we immediately saw a huge sign: 'Restaurant'.

"I'll bet that's it," I said, partly out of relief that my confidence had been well placed that our place of refuge would reveal itself spontaneously and I wouldn't have to find someone to ask.

We entered by the rear entrance, into the dining area which was practically full. It appeared that a large group of holidaymakers were lunching together. We were greeted by a lady who I presumed was the lady of the house, and when I gave our names she nodded in recognition. We lugged our bags through the restaurant into the bar, where the owner himself met us and led us out via a rear door, up a short path, then along another alleyway for twenty metres or so at which point we found ourselves at the top of a short incline leading directly to the harbour. He turned right, and stopped outside the next gateway but one.

"This is my annexe. You're in here."

There was a small breakfast room to the left, and he nipped behind the bar to collect our key.

"It's on the first floor." He held out the key and indicated the stairs.

"OK. Thank you."

And with that he returned to his duties and left us to our own devices.

The rear entrance to our hotel.

Our room had a single and a double bed, and as is customary when Mike and I travel together I always take the left-hand bed and he the right. Don't ask me why!

Beside my bed was a staircase leading to a room overhead, so close that I had to squeeze past it to get to the bed. I set out to explore.

"There's a notice on the wall informing guests that this is a Japanese staircase. What on earth does that mean?"

"No idea. Perhaps you have to go up sideways and it will Tokyo to the upper floor."

"Ha, ha. You mean 'Once you start, you can Nippon up?" No, I'm looking at the treads. They're cut away alternately. It seems that you have to start with the right foot and then the left, because of the way the treads are cut. What's the point?'

"Ask the Japanese."

"I don't think I'll find any here on Molène."

"Probably not. Go on up and see what's up there."

Three more beds, no chairs and hardly room to swing the proverbial feline.

Our lower level accommodation included a bathroom and shower, hanging space for coats, a desk set against the wall and a chair. The chair was distinctive.

"The legs are about a foot too high," I observed, "and the back only goes up as far as my waist. I can't lean against the back of the chair because there's nothing to lean back onto."

We changed places.

"If you try to write at the desk, it's like writing on your knees," Mike said. "It's the sort of device I'd expect to find in a nineteenth century prison cell, designed to chastise the inmate by making writing as uncomfortable as possible."

"I suspect it was bought as a bar stool, where it would have served perfectly well. When a chair was needed for this room, instead of going out and buying one they moved this one in. It's totally unsuitable for a bedroom."

Molène is treeless and more or less both round and flat, the highest point being only 27m above sea level. There is a resident population of about 200, which triples in the summer when holidaymakers arrive. The island's settlement, dominated by the spire of the church, is located on the south-east side facing the picturesque harbour. In the past, the population was three times greater and the local economy was based on fishing. Only a handful of full-time professional fishermen remain.

We deployed to the restaurant for dinner. There was a choice of five main courses, and it occurred to me that if one stayed longer than five days it might become a bit repetitive. The standard of cooking, though, was high. I needed a smoke, but it was raining and I was forced to cower in the doorway of our house. A bit 'back of the bike sheds', I thought.

The following morning called for a plan of action.

"We're here for all day and half of tomorrow. Where shall we start?"

"We're right on the harbour. It's only a hundred yards end to end, and you can take photos of the pleasure craft bobbing in the swell or that large island with the sheds on it on the other side which they say you can access on foot at low water."

A couple of doors along from our billet was an open-air bar with some tables, and when the owner started laying them out it was clear that after sitting and enjoying our coffee, we could then have some lunch without having to stir. All was well until Mike decided to move around to sit facing the harbour and caught his chair leg against the table. His coffee cup went flying and he lost the lot. After buying a replacement and finishing it he wandered off to the jetty to take photos, leaving me lingering over my cup.

"Are you staying to eat?" the owner asked.

"Yes," I said. *"I'm waiting for my friend. He's down on the jetty taking photos."*

I waved to Mike and indicated that he should return and let the café proprietor serve us some lunch.

"Do you want 'moules frites' or 'saucisse de Molène frites'?"

"Is that all there is?"

"Looks like it. But if they've got a local delicacy, their own sausage, it seems churlish not to try it."

It went down well, but it didn't strike me as being distinctive in any way. Maybe my palate isn't sufficiently discerning.

"I suppose we'd better have a wander around."

The houses and gardens were separated by wide paths, some with tarmac, others gravel and others nothing – just grass. With, according to our brochure, only six cars on the island for commercial purposes, there's scarcely any need. The church had a memorial to St Renan, an Irish monk who made landfall c500AD. Following directions, we found the gift shop and the general store, where I bought myself some vacuum-packed Molène sausage to take home.

"What now? We seem to have done the 'grand tour'. It's a quarter past three, and the sun's come out."

The village shop is on the left.

"The brochure mentions a 'round-the-island walk'. I think maybe we do this now in case it rains tomorrow. It mentions some Neolithic remains. We can see if they're worth finding."

Our brochure indicated that the path began at the end of the harbour, but there was no sign saying 'Round-the-Island Path Starts Here' or some such. Open grass later degenerated to mud because the well-trodden way was reduced in width to such an extent that to keep to it meant putting one foot directly in front of the other. Stopping occasionally to admire views of rocks out at sea or a distant lighthouse, we completed the circumambulation in an hour and a half. We noted that, were it to rain, there had been no shelter anywhere.

"Have you noticed that we haven't seen any animals or any signs of farming?" asked Mike.

"Yes. The land's been abandoned to scrub, fern and brambles. If I lived here, I'd have a field turned over to poultry and I'd be keeping the villagers in eggs."

"And as there are no farmyard animals, what do they make this Molène sausage from?"

"If I was bringing a coach party here, I'd be careful to count them in and count them all out. If one was missing... well, that's your answer. What a sales pitch! 'Get your Molène sausage here! Made for tourists! Made *from* tourists!'"

"I don't think. But it remains a bit of a mystery."

We noted a crêperie on the outskirts of the village. 'Lunch tomorrow?'

The following morning, I chanced to glance out of the narrow bedroom window and saw the sea and sky completely calm and the sun's rays from below the horizon turning the underside of the clouds crimson.

"Quick, Mike," I called to my dozing companion. "Grab your camera and catch this wonderful dawn before the sun rises and it changes. It's the stuff of calendars."

After breakfast, the only guests, we packed and deposited our luggage in the bar before setting off into the village once more, this time to visit the semaphore tower, no longer in use but preserved as a tourist attraction and open 7/7 from 9 a.m. We arrived at 10h30 to find it firmly locked. We walked back down past the school, and an elderly lady in her front garden kindly directed us to the cistern for catching rainwater which we were trying to find. Our own Queen Victoria funded it in recognition of the bravery of the island's fishermen in 1896 in attempting to rescue passengers and crew of the S.S. Drummond Castle. The safe passage past Ushant is to the north, but for some reason the captain tried to sail south between Ushant and Molène, hit a rock and the ship sank in four minutes with almost total loss of life.

My next destination was the souvenir shop to buy some cards and stamps, then off to find the post office before it closed at midday for the weekend and then on to track down that *crêperie* we'd noted yesterday. To my delight it offered a full menu of my favourite galettes.

Nothing now but to return to the hotel to sit with our luggage over a drink and mark time till the ferry arrived at 17h30. In two-and-a-half days I think we'd totally exhausted the attractions of Molène, added to which the weather was turning dank and miserable.

I thought to myself: "I've ticked another French island off the list, with the usual caveat that I never expect to visit it again. The people were uniformly cheerful and pleasant, but there is nothing of interest to bring anyone here unless you're a sailor revelling in testing your skills against the hidden dangers of the local waters, with their rip tides, currents and submerged rocks to add to the Atlantic swell and changeable weather."

Along with other passengers on the exposed jetty we huddled in the drizzle as the ferry hove into view. It was, I'm afraid, rather thankfully, goodbye to Molène.

NB Soon after returning home I wrote to the mayor's office asking where the animals were from which *'saucisse de Molène'* was made. I did not receive a reply.

Postscript

I was sitting in the lounge alone in the house when I heard the phone ring in the hall. As I picked it up, I heard a click as someone upstairs picked up the extension.

That's funny, I thought. I'm alone in the house, and in any case, I haven't got an extension upstairs.

What's even stranger, I live in a bungalow. Strangest of all, I haven't got a phone.

And to you, dear reader,

Goodnight.

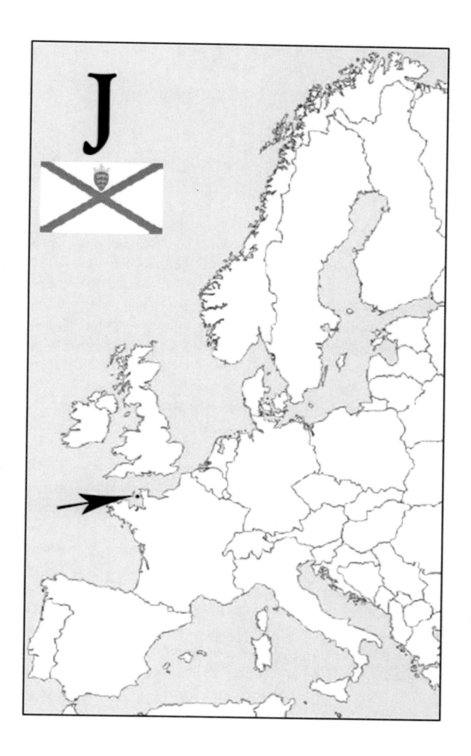

Jersey
Waving, Not Drowning

In my young days, all physically fit young men had to do two years in the armed forces – national service, it was called. There was no escaping it. Once you reached 18 you got your call-up papers and were ordered to report to a barracks and get a short haircut and be kitted out with your uniform. You could defer it if you were an apprentice or going to university, but this meant doing it at a later age and then probably finding, at 21 or 22, being ordered around by an NCO was even more distasteful than it would have been at 18. I was determined to get into the navy when my time came, partly through being born in Portsmouth, a major naval base, and partly through being brought up by my grandparents. Pa had been a chief engine room artificer in Queen Victoria's navy and 'done his twenty-two'[1]. When I was a small boy, he'd told me countless stories of his time on the Far East Station and sailing up the Yangtse and through the Suez Canal. His own grandfather had been Nelson's coxswain at the Battle of Copenhagen in 1801. All this had inspired me to want to follow in his footsteps should the opportunity arise.

The way to ensure one got into the navy rather than the army or air force was to join the Royal Naval Volunteer Reserve (RNVR). This was possible from the age of 17 and I was still in the sixth form at school when a few weeks after my birthday I took the train to Southampton Docks to join up.

I passed the medical, A1, and was then asked which branch I wanted to join. I chose VS, visual signals. To be accepted for that branch required an eyesight test to ensure that the applicant had perfect colour vision, because obviously if he couldn't distinguish the colours of the flags, he wouldn't be able to read them.

Once training started, I was taught morse code so as to be able to send messages at sea using a lamp and had to learn the semaphore alphabet in order to make signals with a flag in each hand, spelling out the letters. Both systems were terribly slow, sending a message one letter at a time. The other challenge was to memorise the flag alphabet and know which letter they represented and what meaning they had when hoisted at the yardarm singly, or in combination with others.

Recruits had to learn how to march in step, how to hold a rifle on the shoulder and how to present arms. The Admiral Commanding Reserves (ACR) inspected each RNVR station once a year, and was met by a guard of honour made up of new recruits, carrying their rifles. The tallest new entry was detailed to be right hand marker, which meant marking time on parade acting as the pivot while the rest of the guard of honour moved into line. This distinction fell to me as I was officially measured at 6' 0½". Quite daunting for a raw 17-year-old. Make a wrong move, and the parade would end up in disarray in front of the admiral and guess who would look like a right idiot...

All members of the RNVR had to attend a minimum number of evenings in a year, known as 'divisions'. For me, this meant changing out of my school uniform into my naval uniform and catching the bus one stop down Portsdown Hill to the railway station at Cosham, get off at Woolston, take the floating bridge across the River Itchen to Southampton and then walk half a mile or so to the docks, where the training ship was berthed. Coming back, I got to Cosham just in time to catch the last bus home to Clanfield, arriving home at a quarter to midnight. I did this for two years while at school studying for my A levels or working in my first job in Portsmouth Dockyard, before the envelope bearing the legend 'On Her Majesty's Service' eventually hit the mat and I was called up.

'Divisions' were held on Mondays and Thursdays, and it was up to each of us to decide whether to attend once a week throughout the year or go twice and take a break when we'd reached our required quota. So long as you'd attended the minimum number of 'divisions' you got your pay and travelling expenses and appropriate entries in your service record, gaining seniority and qualifying for promotion.

An additional annual requirement was to serve for a fortnight in the Royal Navy proper, either in a naval shore station or aboard a sea-going ship. One year I was sent to HMS *Osprey* in Weymouth for the first week to hone my skills with an aldis lamp, a hand-held box with a lamp inside, worked by pulling a trigger to make it flash. For the second week, I was posted to a destroyer to get experience of life at sea for real. On board this ship a 16st three-badge AB[2] with arms covered in tattoos took me under his wing and showed me how to sling a hammock and stow it away in the morning (yes, the lower deck still slept in hammocks aboard ship in those days). Later that day, seeing that I had a hole in one of my socks, he got out his 'hussiff' ('housewife'), a rolled pocket made of cloth and containing wool and needles and showed me how to darn it. It may sound positively antediluvian to a modern reader when I confess that I still darn my socks when necessary thanks to that burly three-badge AB, and still have the 'hussiff' I was issued with when I was first kitted out, still with my name stamped on it in white paint.

In mid-Channel we undertook various exercises, such as rescuing a hand who'd fallen overboard (a volunteer would jump over the side and pretend to be drowning). In my case it enabled me to practise my skills hoisting signals on the yardarm and reading the reply signalled by the ship ahead or astern. In the navy, signal flags are called 'bunting', and lower deck slang for those of us who hoisted them aloft was 'bunting tossers', just as a wireless operator was known as 'sparks' and the chap who prepared our breakfast was 'chef' or 'cookie'.

We found a quite different name for ours on one occasion, though. We were out in mid-Channel when chef brought in a metal jug containing a quart of hot kye[3] and put it on the messdeck table. We all gathered around with our mugs and he filled them and left us to enjoy it in peace. The first man drank half a mug, yelled and shot up the companion way (ladder) to the upper deck and rushed to the side, spewing his ring, as we say. 'Chef' had made the cocoa and put in plenty of white crystals to sweeten it. But had picked up the wrong basin. It wasn't sugar he'd stirred in, but salt. Aaaaargh! He ended up in the rattle[4], but that was small compensation.

Our RNVR station had the use of four MLs, motor launches, approximately 112ft overall and with a draught of 13ft. At sea, I was always up on the open bridge with the captain and navigating officer, as at any time there might be an emergency and he'd need his signalman beside him to take orders for a signal to be hoisted. Or one of the other ships would hoist one and he'd need me to be at hand to read it. For an 18-year-old to be out at sea and on the bridge alongside the skipper was an exhilarating experience and I was the envy of my schoolmates when I was back in class the next week telling them all about it. OK, yeah, I guess you're right. Bragging.

Our ML entering harbour.

As well as the fortnight's training, we also had the opportunity to go to sea for long weekends over Easter and Whitsun and cross the Channel to tie up alongside in a French port such as Cherbourg or in one of the Channel Islands. It was one such training weekend which took me to Jersey, where my principal memory is of being on middle watch, 12 midnight to 4 a.m.

The islands in this part of the Channel are renowned for the difference between high and low water, a matter of approximately 15m (45ft). This meant that the two of us on watch, instead of sitting on the bridge having a chat while keeping a casual eye on the dockside for any unauthorised visitors we had to go for'ard to slacken off the mooring ropes to prevent them snapping under the weight of the ship as it dropped with the tide, then go aft and repeat the exercise. By the time we'd done that it was time to go for'ard and slack off again, and so on, almost continuously through our watch. It was freezing cold at that time of night and we were glad to be relieved after four hours and get to our bunks and get warm again.

One tale I tell scares the daylights out of most people, even today. On a bright sunny day, well out of sight of land the captain asked me if I was competent with semaphore. I assured him that I was, whereupon he handed me a short note and instructed me to send it to the ship ahead. This meant that I had to go as far for'ard as was possible in order to be visible from the other vessel and then make semaphore for the signalman on that ship, standing in the stern, to read.

There was a snag. To send semaphore, you need both arms free to hold the flags. How, then, do you keep steady on a ship at sea? Answer: right at the bow is the jackstaff, on which a flag is flown when in harbour. The skipper instructed me to wrap my legs around this and grip it as tightly as possible with my knees and this would leave my arms free to send the message. On this occasion, although the sea conditions were calm, we were, after all, in the middle of the English Channel and there was a bit of an Atlantic swell. As a result, with the ship rising and falling about 20 feet and rolling through about ten degrees there was me, gripping the jackstaff with might and main between my knees while plunging down and then up while also rolling from side to side, trying to keep both arms free to send a message. Having done that, I had to steady myself along the guardrail and return to the bridge and be ready with pad and pencil to read the reply sent back in semaphore by the other ship and pass it to the captain.

It was only an exercise. Knowing this, I don't recall being scared, merely exhilarated. But in a real situation in wartime a signalman would be expected to be able to carry out such an operation and as all the officers had seen active service during the war, I'm pretty sure they'd done this for real at some time or other and possibly even under enemy fire. Us youngsters who'd been too young to serve in the war were undergoing training in case there was another one – World War 3. At that time the 'cold war' was at its most intense and Stalin was still alive, so who knew what the future might hold?

When I've related this story to my friends, they've always asked me what the hell the skipper was doing exposing me to such danger. My riposte is that I had confidence that, in ordering me to undertake this exercise, the captain was well aware of the risks but wouldn't have considered that I was in danger of serious injury or death by drowning. For my part, I was 18 and at the age when young men think they're invincible and indestructible and I enjoyed the challenge and gained in self-confidence through meeting it. My friends have also always concurred that nowadays Health and Safety would have a fit!

While in harbour, 'hands' not on watch took turns at having what's called in naval slang 'a run ashore'. A group of us shipmates, about half-a-dozen, went into St Helier to seek out a cheap café for some grub followed by a pub crawl before returning to the ship a bit the worse for wear. Drunkenness, however, was contrary to KR & AI (King's Regulations and Admiralty Instructions) and penalties were harsh. The argument was that a sailor is 'a fighting man' and must always be ready to carry out his duties. If he was unfit through drink then he wouldn't be in a fit state to fight so wasn't justifying his pay. We all knew the rules and I don't recall any of us ever drinking so much that we were incapable.

I enjoyed my two-and-a-half years in the RNVR prior to being called up. When that happened, I was far better prepared for life in the armed forces than the other 18-year-olds who came in straight from school or from their jobs if they'd left school at 14. Some of them had the utmost difficulty making the transition from civilian life to service life. But that's another story.

National service turned boys into men, capable of getting out of bed on command, shaving in cold water, getting dressed and on parade and able to obey orders without hesitation. Through being thrown together cheek by jowl, out of necessity we learned to develop comradeship with people from totally different backgrounds who, when they came from different parts of the country, often had barely intelligible accents.

By learning to accept discipline and to obey a higher rank you also learned self-discipline: how to keep your mouth shut when given an order you didn't agree with. An order was an order not a negotiating position, and your valuable opinion was not required. The boys who learned that lesson grew up and became men, and from that character transition they, their family and their friends benefited for the rest of their lives.

That, at least, was my experience. Sadly, young people today don't have the opportunity that my generation had, and are the poorer for it.

Easter 1951

Aged 17, Boy Signalman.

Aged 25, Sub-Lieutenant (Special Branch).

Postscript

All the crew were civilians, and the officers, though highly experienced because they'd served during the war, had long since been demobbed and were office workers, architects, solicitors and so on. The only full-time professional was the shipkeeper, an old 'regular' who'd finished his time but then been taken on to maintain the ship in dock and be there on hand when at sea.

I remember with great affection one such, Harry Muncey, who once overheard someone refer to him as 'a silly old bastard' to which he took great, but mock, exception, saying, "I don't mind someone calling me a bastard, but I'm not going to be called 'old'."

While keeping a completely straight face, he told me the tale of a signalman who was lost at sea because a flag snagged on the yardarm and the skipper sent him aloft to free it and he took so long doing it that when he came down again the ship had gone.

Guide to Naval Slang

1. 'done his 22'. Served in the navy for 22 years and retired with a full pension.
2. 'three-badge AB'. An able seaman with fifteen years' service, who had either not sought or not gained promotion. The 'badge' was a chevron on the left upper arm, one awarded for each 5 years' service with good conduct (with a maximum of three). On working clothes, it was red, but on dress uniform gold.
3. 'kye'. Cocoa. Pronounced 'kigh' as in 'high'.
4. 'in the rattle'. Up in front of the captain on a charge of misconduct.

Goodnight.

St Brelades Bay.

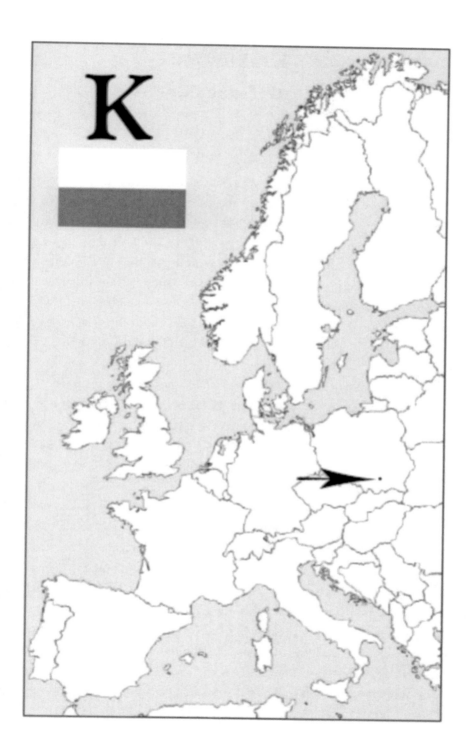

K

Kraków*

Separate Honeymoons

On my first visit to Kraków at the age of 25 I made my first Polish friend, Wacek*. He had aspirations to become a concert pianist and lived in a tiny two-roomed flat – more like one room plus walk-in cupboard for a kitchen, dominated by his grand piano. After I returned to England we corresponded regularly, and he invited me to come over again and stay with him. In those days to get a visa to go to Poland was only possible if you had an invitation and even then, there was no certainty that it would be granted. I was, naturally, keen to accept, but had to admit that it might not be as straightforward as it had been before when I was being sponsored by an organisation which applied for the visas en bloc.

"Wacek, yes, I'd love to come and stay with you. But there's a problem."

"What?"

"I've just got married. If I come now, I shall want to bring my wife."

"I haven't got room for both of you. If she comes she'll have to stay with someone else. I'll see if I can find someone who can put her up."

So, it transpired that having got married in the April and put off having a proper honeymoon until the school summer holidays, we ended up spending it in separate flats, half a mile apart.

Wacek met us at the station and took us back to his flat. I was to have his bed, while he'd doss underneath the grand piano. Margaret was to stay with his friend Renata, who fortunately was a teacher of English at a commercial college. She had, by Polish standards of the time, a large flat including a bed space for the home help to look after her two children while she was at work. By packing them and the maid off to her mother in the country, she could offer Margaret a bit of privacy – which she appreciated as she was by now two months pregnant. Moreover, Rena was delighted to have the opportunity to practise her spoken English and, as Wacek wasn't much of a cook, she would provide us with dinner in the evenings. Her husband, Władek*, was also very hospitable, and was able to talk to his house guest, Margaret, in German.

This being a family holiday and knowing that Polish families had a hard struggle to make ends meet, we had every intention of paying our way. So, most mornings we went shopping for food for the evening meal. Lunch was sometimes taken in a restaurant and was a bit of a culture shock. Wacek's establishment of choice was called 'Kapusta' *, which means 'cabbage'. This struck me as a very direct, no-nonsense name to give to a restaurant. Hardly imaginative, eh? Not even 'Leafy Cabbage' or 'Spring Cabbage'; just 'Cabbage'. But then it wasn't privately owned, but state-run. So, who cares what it's called? Take it, or leave it. What's it to me whether you come again or not?

It was the first time we'd ever eaten cherry soup, served cold. But in the height of summer, it was agreeably refreshing. On one occasion, we'd just had some fish, and an old crone came up behind me and muttered something unintelligible in my ear and then leaned over my shoulder and scooped up the fish bones and heads off my plate and stuffed them into her mouth. Wacek explained that she was a poor woman with no money to buy food, and the only way she could get anything to eat was to scrape up the leavings off diners' plates. As you will not be surprised to hear, I was totally taken aback by the whole experience.

Another strange custom was that there was no proper queuing system and the waiters didn't see it as part of their job to find you a table. You had to look around the room, decide which of the diners was likely to finish first and then go and stand behind them ready to sit down in their chairs the moment they got up to leave. When you were nearing the end of your own meal, you'd suddenly find someone was standing behind you. It was a bit unnerving trying to finish the dessert course or coffee in a relaxed manner and talk to your table companions while a couple of total strangers hovered behind you rocking from one foot to the other willing you to hurry up and finish and clear off so that they could sit down and have their lunch.

Wacek spoke remarkably good English, considering that he had never been out of Poland and had learned most of it through reading Shakespeare. Some of his phrases were a bit odd, as when for example he referred to 'the blinds'. For the life of us we couldn't understand what was wrong with the curtains and only after much questioning did we realise that what he meant was blind people. Think of it in French: a blind person is 'un aveugle', so surely 'les aveugles' translates as 'the blinds'. No, of course it doesn't. When we went to Ojców* in the foothills of the Tatra Mountains, Wacek pointed out a famous tourist attraction, a great limestone pinnacle which he told us was called 'Hercules' Knob'. We had to gently suggest that perhaps 'Hercules' Club' would be a more discreet way of putting it, while keeping a straight face.

Wacek and Rena showed us everything Kraków had to offer – and it was a great deal. As the capital of the Polish kings, it had the Wawel* Palace for starters and parts of the original city defences. We were particularly taken by the royal council chamber and the heads of the king's counsellors of state carved in wood and mounted in the recesses of the ceiling. Rena obviously told Władek about our interest and when we came to take our leave, he presented us with a parting gift which turned out to be one of these heads. We nicknamed him 'Fred' and to this day he gives everyone who enters my house the once-over from his place of honour above the kitchen doorway facing the front door.

'Fred'

The other great thrill was going up the tower of the fourteenth century St Mary's Basilica, famous for having two towers of different heights. The legend is that the architects were two brothers commissioned to build a tower each, and when the younger one discovered that his brother's tower was going to be higher than his he killed him and then completed his own tower to be the higher. Overcome with remorse, he then climbed to the top, proclaimed his guilt and threw himself off and fell to his death.

The tower of the original church on this site was used as a look-out post and legend has it that a sentry on duty in, it's believed, 1241 saw the invading Mongol army approaching and sounded the alarm for the guards to shut the town's gates. Unfortunately, an arrow through his throat killed him before he could finish. It is a long-established Polish tradition to sound the *hejnal* every hour from a similar position high up in the tower of the present church, stopping in mid-blow in honour of the sentry who perished warning the city. It's a very eerie experience to hear. If you look up you can see the trumpet sticking out of the window and possibly catching the sun's rays.

In contrast, we relaxed in one of the shops under the world-famous market hall, the fifteenth century Sukiennice*, where we discovered they served wild strawberries and cream for the equivalent in our money of fifty pence. Where else can you eat wild strawberries commercially? I enjoy them regularly every summer, not because I know anywhere where I can buy them but because I grow them in my garden amongst my raspberries.

The fifteenth century Sukiennice.

Being pregnant, Margaret had the usual odd cravings for foods and in her case, it was plums and unfortunately oranges. These latter were absolutely unobtainable in Poland in 1960. Wacek explained that once a year a boat docked in Gdańsk to supply the whole country with just one delivery, everyone went down to the shops and bought every last one, children got their first taste – and that was that until the same time next year when the next shipment came in. Oranges occasionally came in from Bulgaria, but this wasn't the season. It reminded me of my childhood during the war when for the duration we had no exotic fruit and no ice cream. The war had been over for fifteen years, but in Poland living standards were still much like war-time Britain.

Plums were no problem, as they were sold at the roadside by peasant women in from the countryside where they grew them. We decided that as Margaret was having a free ride and we were doing all the talking we would help her to become independent and be able to ask for plums for herself. It's not easy in Polish for someone with no previous experience of Slavonic languages, but she eventually got the hang of 'half a kilo of plums, please', which in Polish is *pół kilo śliwek, proszę.*

The first time she tried it, the old lady she addressed not only sold her what she wanted but thanked her in perfect German! The explanation, I said, was that whatever schooling she might have had would have been pre-First World War when this region in Poland was part of the Austro-Hungarian Empire – added to which, the Nazi Occupation had made a knowledge of German a practical necessity. Britain in the 1950s was pretty much a monoglot country, and this chance occurrence in Poland brought home how normal it was on the continent

100

for even people with little formal education to be able as a matter of course to speak more than one language.

In the years immediately following our visit, Wacek and Rena came separately to stay with us in England and I remember the look of total disbelief on Rena's face when for the first time she came shopping with us and saw the variety of goods on offer in our shops. In the years that followed the Polish economy went from bad to worse and when Rena became a grandmother and her daughter couldn't get clothes for a new baby we made up parcels of baby clothes and simple toilet items and sent them using a sort of 'food parcel' system run by the Polish community in Southampton. This consisted of packing gifts in cardboard boxes and putting them on a lorry and taking them to Poland by road. They were subsequently off-loaded at the local post office nearest the addressee, who was then informed that there was a box from England for them to collect.

Many of the baby clothes came from children in our classes at school. We used to ask the class if they had any new brothers or sisters who had outgrown their first bootees or rompers. When we told them what we wanted them for the children would bring them in and we made up our boxes and sent them off to a country where such things were virtually unobtainable. We usually added a few luxuries such as ladies' tights, a box of corn flakes and some chocolate bars. Nothing too heavy, as we had to pay for the transport of our box according to its weight. But it's what friends are for.

We lost touch with Wacek, but Rena stayed in contact with us for the next forty years until, having reached her 80s, the letters stopped. Sadly, her children, Rafael and Maria, never bothered to write to tell us that she'd died, notwithstanding that twenty years before we'd supplied Maria with clothes for her babies in her hour of need.

August 1960

Guide to Pronunciation

kapusta:	*ka-**poo**-sta*
Kraków:	***Krack**-oof*
Ojców:	***Oi**-tsoof*
Puł kilo śliwek, proszę:	*poowl **kee**-la **shleeve**-ek, **pro**-sheh*
Sukiennice:	***Soo**-kyen-ee-tsa*

Wacek:	*Vats-ek*
Wawel:	*Vah-vel*
Władek:	*V-wah-dek*

Postscript

My wife came in from the cold, collapsed into an armchair in the front room by the fireplace, took off her fur hat and dropped it on the hearth. When she went out to hang her coat up, I nipped into the kitchen and got a saucer of milk and put by her fur hat. When she came back into the room, she burst out laughing!

We had dinner in the dining room and went back into the lounge to watch TV.

The hat and the saucer were still there, but the milk had gone.

Goodnight.

We thought this charming wooden fruit bowl from the Tatra Mountains showing a young couple in traditional peasant costume would be a suitable memento of our honeymoon.

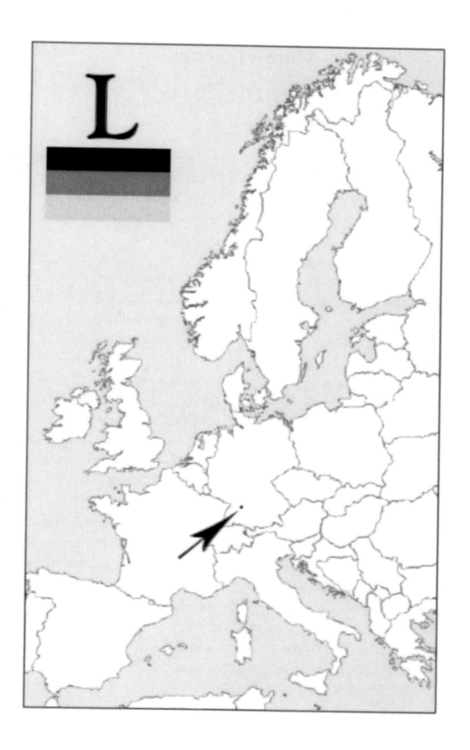

Ludwigsburg
Same Options, Maybe Different Outcomes

I always took a great interest in our borough's twinning with towns in France and Germany and especially the variety of local organisations which exchanged twinning visits independently: doctors, church groups, sportsmen and youth groups, former members of the armed services and especially our carnival committee.

Some schools also took part, but not as much as we would have liked. This was because the initiative lay with the language staff, who had spent their study time abroad in various other towns. They preferred to take their pupils to where they already knew the area and probably had friends, rather than going to the borough's twin towns with which they were not familiar and where they didn't know anybody.

For many years I served on the governing body of Tankerville, our local school for severely mentally handicapped children. To be precise it was eighteen years, with twelve as chairman, and the idea occurred to me: why shouldn't we 'twin'? It was taken for granted that 'normal' children from 'normal' schools could go on foreign exchanges, but no one had ever seriously considered such a thing for mentally handicapped youngsters. Would it be possible? Would it be worth the effort?

The situation was made easier by a stroke of luck: Ute*, our school secretary, was a German lady, long settled in this country due to her former marriage to an Englishman. This meant that we would have no problems in corresponding with Kornwestheim, our German twin town. On one of my official visits in my other capacity as a borough councillor I enquired of our hosts what provision they made for educating handicapped children. I was told that they were sent to a special school in Ludwigsburg, the regional capital, a few miles away. I ascertained the address and correspondence ensued.

To cut a long story short, the Principal of the school was delighted to see what could be arranged to promote a 'twinning' arrangement and exchange visits with us. Our first personal contact came when I called on him the next time I was in Kornwestheim and invited him to come over to meet us, see our school and bring some of his staff. They spoke English at various levels of proficiency and we got along famously.

The main problem was that our schools were not exactly matched. We only had children up to the statutory school leaving age, who were with us primarily because of mental handicap though perhaps had some physical disabilities in addition. In Germany, the school provided permanent day-time education and training for a slightly older age group, and also for those with more profound physical handicaps than those in our school. But if we wanted to 'twin', this was the nearest match we would get.

Our children's parents were delighted with the suggestion. Those who could afford to pay the entire costs did so willingly and we found ways of helping out those who couldn't. We had to be very selective about who we took, because they'd be away from home – usually for the first time in their lives – and living with a strange family during their stay. There would inevitably be a language barrier, but it was quite a revelation to discover how determined our pupils were – severely mentally handicapped, remember – to learn some German phrases. Not a lot, of course – some of them could barely make themselves understood in English. But they wanted to 'give it a go', helped by Ute.

The host families were chosen on the basis that they had handicapped children of their own and so knew what to expect. They would have a house guest who was much like their own child, requiring much the same sort of care and assistance during their stay which they were used to providing anyway.

The school itself in Ludwigsburg was quite remarkable in its concept. Horst, the Principal, complained about lack of funding, telling us that the regional government had put a mint of money into building a state-of-the-art school and equipping it, then more or less washed its hands of further financial support. If one of the staff was ill, he couldn't phone up for a temporary replacement. In other words, he couldn't get what in English schools we call 'supply cover'. He just had to cope as best he could.

His buildings and equipment were, however, far superior to ours and many of the classrooms had doors opening onto individual secure outdoor areas where the young people could spend part of the day in the fresh air, whether in a class or during a recreation period. Many of those who attended were young adults in their twenties, whereas our children left us at sixteen. We were hugely impressed to discover that the school caretaker had his own vineyard and were quite overcome by his generosity when on our departure he proudly presented each of us with a bottle of wine made from his own grapes.

As chairman of governors I accompanied the exchange, so I know how well it turned out. We struck up friendships with the staff and visited some of them in their own homes. Eva*, the Deputy Principal, lived in a neighbouring village, Besigheim, in a traditional Swabian half-timbered house with the date '1598' over the door. Every room was full of junk and her husband Matthias*, an artist, just got on with his work utterly unfazed.

Ludwigsburg itself is a fine city, famous for producing delicate hand-painted porcelain. In the eighteenth century when Württemberg was independent it was the ducal capital and had a palace, Schloss Ludwigsburg, to match. They took us on a tour, amusing us by showing us the table out of which a semi-circle had been cut to accommodate the royal stomach: King Friedrich I (1805–16) as well as measuring 4m (13ft) around the waist, stood 2.08m tall (that's about 6'10" in old money) and weighed over 30 stone. This caused considerable embarrassment to Napoleon when he negotiated, as the Emperor was only 1.68m (5'6") and didn't take kindly to being so totally dwarfed by his ally.

Schloss Ludwigsburg.

They also told us that in 1812 King Friedrich supplied Napoleon with 16,000 soldiers for the invasion of Russia, of whom only a few hundred came back. I think in modern times a mortality rate in the military of 95% would cause questions in parliament. Ah! – 'the good old days'!

Was the exchange worth it for our children? Most if not all are still around, so one could ask them. I'm confident that their memories would be positive. I took the view that 'inclusion' is not a matter of sending all children to the same schools and even less is it a question of ruling out certain subjects or topics on the grounds that they are not 'relevant' and everyone gets the same curriculum. It's a question of giving all children equal opportunities.

I'm forever glad such patronising nonsense wasn't in fashion when I was a boy. I lived deep in the Hampshire countryside and was being brought up by a widowed grandmother. My education, however, was not restricted to 'useful' subjects befitting a working-class boy whose family had neither connections nor money, but included English literature, French and Latin. In what way were foreign languages, least of all dead ones, 'relevant' to me with my likely path in life?

The assumption at my grammar school was that all the boys went either into the civil service or the armed forces, unless they came from the villages and preferred to stay put and work on the land or, in my village, opted for the local brewery. If they didn't fancy any of these, the other main source of employment was Portsmouth Dockyard. Girls, of course, worked in shops or offices until they got married and then spent the rest of their lives caring for children, waiting hand and foot on their husband in gratitude for him bringing home his wages and being tied to a gas stove (or maybe a paraffin heater if gas hadn't yet reached their village). Like I just said – ah! – 'the good old days'!

So why should our special education kids miss out? If visits to the continent were a good thing for 'normal' kids, who's to say ours, who were not 'normal', wouldn't also benefit although perhaps not in exactly the same ways? I saw it as a question of affording all children equal respect and providing them as far as possible with the same opportunities, varied to take account of each individual's mental and physical capacities.

I distanced myself from the official view which routinely underestimated them or assumed that they couldn't do something without trying it out to see if in fact they could – even if only after a fashion. A profoundly handicapped little boy may not say 'Guten Tag' with a very good German accent but, in the instance I'm thinking of, it gave him enormous pleasure to learn to do it at all and he greatly enjoyed the support and encouragement when he said it *in situ* to a

German boy for the first time and was understood. It's difficult enough for ordinary kids to cope with foreign languages or living as house guests in foreign countries, so the achievement of our 'special' kids was that much more to be applauded.

February 1989

Guide to Pronunciation

Eva:	*Eh*-va
Matthias:	*Matt*-yass
Ute:	*OO*-ta

Postscript

Pupil:	"Please, Sir, my pen's run out."
Teacher:	"Run after it, then."

Goodnight.

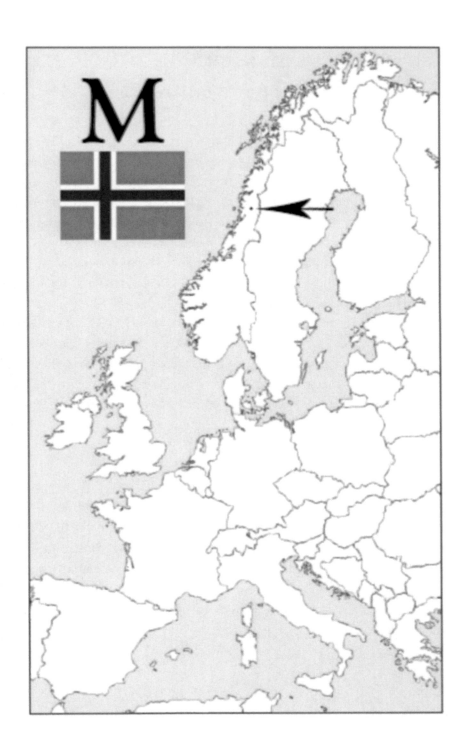

Majavatn*
Unloved, But Not Uneaten

Mike and I had been thumbing away conscientiously all morning outside the little youth hostel at Brekkvasselv, but were stuck. There was just no traffic. About four cars an hour: one the postman, two locals out shopping with whom a lift would only take us a couple of miles, then a tourist's car chock-full of passengers and luggage. Tourists coming south you could always recognise. They invariably had a set of reindeer antlers tied onto the roof of the car, making it look as though the car was head down, charging you. Bought at some Lapp roadside stall, no doubt.

A telegraph linesman whom we'd met at Brekkvasselv took us 40 km up to a lake, Majavatn, where there was another hostel, but that was it. Our best bet looked to be a Volkswagen dormobile with GB plates and only two passengers, but despite passing us and our Union Jack on the roadside twice, at both Brekkvasselv and again at Majavatn, they ignored us. Nothing for it, book ourselves into that youth hostel.

Easy? Routine?

Not up here. Things turned nasty.

Outside the hostel was a car with its bonnet open, giving all the appearance of running repairs being done although there was no one around. We'd been thumbing from outside the hostel for over an hour, and felt sure that the warden or whoever staffed the place must have seen us, seen our flag so known where we came from and probably overheard us talking in English. We approached the door in a spirit of disappointment at our lack of success in getting a lift, though puzzled at the total absence of any signs of life since we'd got out of the linesman's van.

We knocked.

No response.

Again.

Nothing.

Louder.

Still nothing.

Hearing the sound of a vehicle on the road heading north, we nipped back to the roadside hoping that our luck might have changed.

But it hadn't.

Back to the hostel door. Knock, knock.

Bang!

Thump!

Still nothing.

It was beginning to get dark, so quick discussion.

"What do we do if we can't get admitted? It may be listed as a hostel, but maybe they get so few customers they don't bother to open unless someone's booked in advance and as no one has they've gone off visiting friends in Sweden or something."

But no, it wasn't after all a land-based version of the Marie Celeste. There was a sudden bang and we turned around to see a man who'd just slammed the car bonnet shut and was now striding up the steps to the front door. But he took no notice of us at all, not even a glance in our direction. He closed the door behind him.

We waited for the lights to go on. But they didn't.

We went back to the door and knocked – hard. No response. Whoever he was, he wasn't going to answer the door. Not even to make some bogus claim – 'We're full' – or to pointedly suggest that we just bugger in the direction of off.

It was by now nearly dark, we were hungry (you can't prepare food when thumbing), but it looked as though our only option now was to camp out for the night. There was a nice-looking dry spot under some pines down by the shores of Lake Majavatn, so here goes!

Sounds easy, which it is if you've been a scout and know the rudiments. We grew up during the war – no scouts, 'cos no scout leaders – all called up to fight. It also helps if you've got the gear. What tent? What primus? We'd set off to hitch-hike and go *overnatting* (to use the Norwegian term) in youth hostels, not camp. But needs must. At least we had groundsheets, food and matches (we both smoked pipes). We gathered firewood and boiled some water from the lake (after all, Majavatn was a lake) and made mugs of coffee. No milk, but what the heck. We had some sugar, purloined from a roadside café during a comfort stop.

We settled down in our sleeping bags and soon fell asleep. It'd been an exhausting day, because even if you don't get a lift you still have to stand at the roadside and watch out for every approaching vehicle just in case it's the one and if the driver stops be ready to get in there and then. You can't relax, strip off or lay out a picnic. Either you're ready to embark pronto, or just give it up and walk. It's good of the driver to stop at all. He's not going to wait with the engine running while you get dressed, finish your lunch and re-pack your rucksack.

No one had stopped all day, but we'd try again on the morrow. Dawn came, I woke up – alone! Where's Mike? Sleeping bag still there, no him. Trolls spirited him away to Valhalla? I looked out over the lake, beyond which rose a conical mountain the spitting image of those postcards you see of Mount Fuji in Japan. Wreaths of smoke were rising in the foreground, but I couldn't see the source. Until I stood up. Mike was sitting at the water's edge gazing out over the lake and smoking his pipe but with both feet shin-deep in the water.

"What's up?"
"I couldn't get a wink of sleep, so I gave up."
"What was the problem?"
"Mosquitoes."

It transpired that Mike had got so hot in his sleeping bag that he'd got dressed including his socks and lain on top of the bag to cool off. He'd heard the buzzing of the mosquitoes and had felt a stinging sensation, but had decided that the former generated the idea of the latter and had phlegmatically decided to put mind over matter and ignore it.

After some time, matter overcame mind and when he looked at his ankles he saw that both were covered in a swarm of mosquitoes which had alighted on his socks and were sticking their proboscis through the wool and having a good feed – stinging the while! It was at this point that he'd got up and taken to the water, so to speak, and had lit his pipe in the hope that the resultant smoke would discourage them and he'd get some relief. The mozzies didn't like the tobacco smoke, so they stopped attacking him. The water offered a modicum of relief from the score or so of bites each ankle had sustained, but if the only way to keep them away was to smoke then of course he couldn't go back to sleep – you can't sleep and smoke at the same time.

They hadn't touched me. Maybe they knew better than to tangle with a former vice-captain of the team which a couple of years before had won the Inter-Universities Halitosis Challenge Cup, but more to the point I hadn't left any part of my body exposed. Hood of sleeping bag pulled down over the eyes, a handkerchief over the nose and mouth and only a very desperate mosquito is going to get at my chin through that and a thick beard!

We'd covered only 40 km in a whole day, and North Cape was looking as far off come the evening as it had in the morning. But it hadn't been a day without incident.

Better luck tomorrow, eh? Narvik or bust.

But that's a different letter, as you'll find under 'N' (not here, but in my *Little Blue Nightbook*).

August 1959

Guide to Pronunciation

Majavatn: *My-ya-vat-n*

Postscript

A pharmaceutical company received the following letter, endorsing their product.

Dear Sirs,

Before using your ointment, I had a large wart on the back of my hand. I have now been using the cream for six months. The wart is still there, but my hand has completely disappeared.

Yours truly,

Goodnight.

Reindeer grazing beside the road north.

NARVA

Castles in the Air

Estonia's third city is also its most easterly point, right on the frontier with Russia. It's always been that way. In the mid-thirteenth century the Danes occupied the southern shore of the Gulf of Finland and founded a settlement at Reval (the old name for Tallinn) and built a castle on the bank of the river Narva to defend their growing empire. Two-and-a-half centuries later the Russians built one on the opposite bank, barely a quarter of a mile distant. Both are still there, heavily restored and facing each other as they always did. 'East meets West'. Or rather, didn't. It was a stand-off. Maybe it still is?

Mike and I arrived in Narva from St Petersburg, and were the only foreigners to alight from the train when it crossed the frontier. From the Russian border town of Ivangorod* to Narva is only a couple of miles, and we couldn't work out why it was scheduled to take over an hour. The reason was very simple: Estonia operates in a different time zone to Russia. That hour was the adjustment. The actual travelling time from one frontier post to the other was six minutes.

The railway station at Narva.

116

To describe the railway station at Narva as one-horse would be an insult to our equine friends. We alighted on a wooden platform between the tracks and open to the elements, then had to walk back behind the train, down three wooden steps with no ramp alongside for anyone with a bicycle, a pram or, perish the thought, a wheelchair, then down another wooden ramp onto the track, step over the rails to reach another wooden walkway between the lines and finally up a matching ramp to the station platform. All of this while carrying or dragging our suitcases in a temperature of approximately 30°C.

Immigration control consisted of two kiosks, but only one was manned. A benign-looking and rather elderly immigration officer was confronting a queue of no more than half-a-dozen passengers who'd arrived from Russia. I guessed they all lived locally. Except, of course, us – the only foreigners.

I proffered my passport. He looked at my Russian visa and then, with a smile, handed it back.

Turning to Mike, I muttered, "Did you notice something?"

"What?"

"He didn't stamp it."

"Meaning?"

"Estonia is a member of the EU. So are we in Britain. As EU citizens, our passports act as ID and don't require stamping. I'd have liked a souvenir, but in a strange way I feel I'm coming 'home'. Russia is an alien land where their government insists on visas and charges the earth for them. In a funny sort of way Estonia is 'one of us', even though it's a thousand miles from home and I can't speak a word of the language."

After a contrasting but essentially interesting day, we settled for dinner in the hotel rather than going out in an unfamiliar town to look for a restaurant.

Lampreys were listed on the menu, which made our choice easy. Despite what allegedly happened to King John in 1216, we both wanted to try them for the first time. The fish starter included smoked salmon and cod as well as the lampreys. Not a conspicuously unique gastronomic experience, but I can add it to the list of unusual things I've eaten and lived to tell the tale.

"Main course?"

"It says here 'battered butterfish."

"Serves it right for resisting."

"Ha bloody ha. I've never heard of it. I'll give it a try."

It was, as it turned out, excellent. Unfortunately, I no longer have the gargantuan capacity to eat which I had as a young man and was forced to leave half of it. My loss, not the chef's fault.

Despite the hour, it was still stinking hot. We were anxious to get outside onto the terrace for coffee. It also meant that I could indulge in my customary post-prandial cigar and unwind after a fairly eventful day, which had begun with a canal trip in the middle of St Petersburg and had ended with coffee on a quiet terrace in a hotel on the other side of the border in a country which was new to both of us. We looked forward with heightened expectancy to what the next few days would bring. A new country with an unfamiliar history and an incomprehensible language.

Watching the staff about their business, I turned to Mike. "Is it just me, or is there something different about the hotel workers? I know they're the first Estonians we've ever seen and as we've only been here a couple of hours I'd hate to rush to judgment. But there's something intangible at odds with the atmosphere we experienced in Russia, something different in the ambience."

"No, you're right, there is. I can't put my finger on it, either."

"Is it simply because they're speaking a language I can't understand, whereas we've just arrived from a country where, at least some of the time, I could? No, it's not that. There's something about the manner in which they work, all hustle and bustle and 'business-like'.

Sitting here watching the other guests and waiting for our food to arrive, somehow although in my head I know we're not in Russia because we left this afternoon, somehow, I also feel that I'm not in Russia. They seem to be Europeans in a way the Russians weren't. Looking at these blonde waitresses we could be in a restaurant in Holland or Denmark. What is it about them?

"In some indefinable way, they're just different from Russians. They're ethnically different, certainly," I went on to explain.

"They're not Slavs like the Russians, but a Finnic people. That would account for some physiological differences. But that's not it. Why, despite not understanding a word of the language, do I feel in some strange way 'at home' which I didn't in Russia?"

"I think it was encapsulated when that Estonian immigration officer smiled and handed back your passport without stamping it."

"Yes. That gesture said a lot, even without him actually saying a word. It was somehow symbolic. On a more practical note, the menu is priced in euros. They got rid of their national currency last year. They're now integrated with most of the rest of the EU, which may account in a small way for us feeling 'at home'."

The following morning, we planned to visit the castle, our main reason for breaking our journey. We could see it from our hotel window, so clearly it wasn't far away.

"Can you book us an English-speaking guide?" I asked reception.

The receptionist made a phone call. "You can have a guide at eleven o'clock."

We took coffee at an outside table to await his – or her – arrival.

Eleven o'clock arrived, but our guide didn't.

"How long shall we give him?" Mike asked.

"Another five minutes?" I suggested.

At ten past I went in to see reception.

"We're supposed to be having a guide at eleven, but no one's turned up."

"He's at the castle."

"What! I thought he was meeting us here."

"No. At the castle."

At no time had the receptionist mentioned anything about us having to find our own way to the castle in order to meet up with our English-speaking guide. It was a simple case of mutual assumptions. When I asked for the services of a guide, I assumed he or she would come to the hotel and meet us and take us there. The receptionist took my request to mean that I wanted to have a guide available at the castle when we got there.

"Which way is the castle?"

"Turn left, and left again."

"Thank you."

The castle tower was in full view, but when we walked along the road leading to the frontier intending to turn off when we came parallel with the tower we found that there was no access. The area was surrounded by a 5m high wire security fence to control border traffic and enable lorries to be inspected.

Narva Castle.

Retracing our steps, and with no helpful fingerposts pointing the way to the 'Castell' (Estonian for 'castle'), we ended up stumbling our way behind a block of flats through dustbins and parked cars before finally locating the gateway to the castle bailey. By the time we'd crossed to the entrance to the castle itself it was nearly midday and the guide had, not unreasonably, got tired of waiting and gone home, doubtless muttering under his breath about 'perfidious Albion' and bloody foreigners who booked him and then didn't turn up.

"Let's find the ticket office."

"Two euros each."

There was plenty to see in the castle with display cabinets and atmospheric restoration. But the absence of explanations in English rammed home how right we'd been to seek the services of a specialist guide and brought home the extent to which the mix-up at the hotel had left us stranded. Explanations in Estonian are no use to foreign tourists, and no audio cassettes or hand-held printed guides were provided. I could read the gist of explanatory labelling if it was in Russian, but that was of no use to Mike.

"Fine views from here," I said, as we reached the top of the tower.

The look-out platform was completely enclosed in wooden walls and was roofed, and what in earlier times had been arrow slits or portholes for shooting with a musket were now glassed in for the protection and greater comfort of visitors and tourists.

We could walk around all four sides, as the men on guard duty would have done when it was garrisoned. To the north, Russia, the castle of Ivangorod and a bird's-eye view of the bridge over the River Narva and the commercial and domestic traffic queuing to cross. To the east the shallow river meandered slowly, with children playing on the banks on both sides, some on the opposite side in Russia and those on our side in Estonia. On the Estonian side, I noticed a fairly large, elongated island laid out as a park. To the south and west, a view across the town.

Traffic from Russia entering Estonia and the EU.

Across the river, a few hundred metres distant, lay the imposing castle of Ivangorod, built by Ivan III* in 1492 to defend Muscovy, as Russia was known at that time, from the Knights of the Livonian Order.

The castle at Ivangorod in Russia.

"That castle is built in the style we find in Western Europe," I observed. "I see it's also in the throes of extensive repairs. It looks out of place to us because when we think of Russian architecture, we think of onion domes. Here we have battlements and a keep. Seems funny to see it so close yet it's actually in Russia, and to think that it was built at enormous expense at a time when, due to the advent of gunpowder, castle building in Western Europe was coming to an end."

As if to emphasise the point, a Russian flag was fluttering from one of the towers.

Mike continued to take photos of the scenery and buildings from all angles as we made our way back to the gateway arch.

"Pity there was so little explanation in English," Mike muttered, ruefully. "I couldn't understand much of what we saw. What's the history of the castle?"

"It was built by the Danish King Erik IV in 1246 and exactly a hundred years later Valdemar IV sold it to the Teutonic Knights, known by that time as the Livonian Order. They lost it to the Swedes in fifteen-something, then as a result of the Great Northern War of 1700–21 they, the Swedes, that is, ceded it to Peter the Great and it remained part of the Tsarist Empire until the Bolshevik Revolution in 1917 gave the Baltic States the opportunity to proclaim their independence. It was badly damaged by a Russian air raid in 1944 during the Nazi occupation, so what we've just seen is in fact a reconstruction. It said inside that they've restored it to the way it would have looked in the fourteenth century under the Livonian Knights."

"It looked pretty authentic to me," said Mike. "They've done a good job."

We were scheduled to catch the train to Tallinn in the afternoon, having only stopped in Narva overnight to visit the castle.

"We need to get ourselves back to the hotel and get ready to leave," said Mike.

"That café-bar looks inviting," I said, drawing Mike's attention to an ornate doorway.

In the walkway behind the top of the castle walls was the word 'BAAR'.

"I presume that's Estonian for 'bar', not a reference to sheep?" I mused.

"Humph."

"Surely you mean, 'Baa'?"

"And bah! humbug! to you, too."

"We need some drinks for the journey. We going to be on a domestic train, so I don't suppose it'll have a restaurant car."

"What, then?"

"Beer for you, juice for me. I rather took to that *mors* we drank in Novgorod last week. I see they have bottles of it on the counter for sale."

The 'baar' was, in fact, the constable of the castle's private quarters when the castle was functioning as a fortified line of defence. A flight of stairs led up to the walkway behind the battlements where soldiers would have stood on watch. Nowadays drinkers and diners can sit at tables and enjoy their refreshment with a full view of the castle across the bailey.

We made our way back to the hotel without encountering the difficulties which we'd experienced earlier in the day trying to find the castle. There we concluded our brief stop-over in Narva with lunch, but only managed to secure a main course as there were too many other diners for the staff and kitchen to cope with and service was so slow that by the time we were ready for our dessert it was time for our taxi to the station.

On to Tallinn, Tartu and the island of Saaremaa – but that's another story.

July 2014

[Adapted from 'Jottings from Russia and the Baltic States. Part 1: Russia and Estonia'. Other books are listed inside the front cover.]

Guide to Pronunciation

| Ivan: | *Ee-**van*** |
| Ivangorod: | *Ee-**van**-gor-od* |

Postscript

Think, dear reader, of people you know to whom the following character assessment would apply:

"On the surface he's profound, but deep down he's shallow."

Goodnight

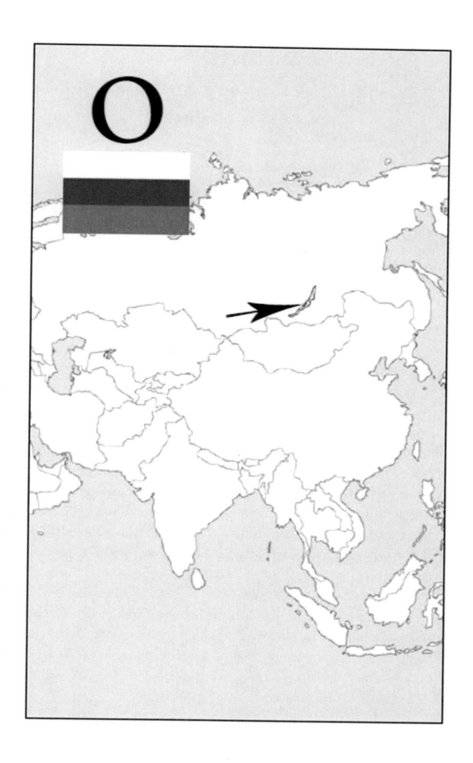

OLKHON*
World-Class Ruts and An Uninvited Guest for Lunch

[Conversations in italics were in Russian]

Crossing Siberia, Mike and I at last reached Lake Baikal. The countryside as we approached the lake was increasingly barren, and other than the fact that there was a road there was no sign of human activity outside the very few villages.

Olkhon came into view at last. At 72x14kms it's the world's third largest island in a lake. Of the total population of 1500, 1200 live in the main settlement, Khuzhir*, where we were headed.

Most of the island was, in fact, uninhabited. You could drive for miles and see nothing but low rolling hills, totally devoid of trees but covered with patches of dry grass with the deep blue of the lake as a backdrop, then perhaps two or three cows or horses but no houses. North of Khuzhir hadn't yet got mains electricity.

On each shore by the landing stages serving the ferry were a few cafés and souvenir stalls, and on the far side low hills dropped steeply down into the lake.

We were last in a queue of five and the tiny ferry, which only took eight or nine cars, was approaching. Olga*, our guide, said that at the height of the season you could be stuck for 24 hours waiting to get across if you hadn't booked. Coming out of season, the length of time we had to wait was minimal. The 1½km ferry section is deemed to be part of the national highway network, so there was no charge. Crossing took about fifteen minutes.

We climbed the companionway above the car deck to enjoy wonderful views of the coast, both of the island and of the mainland behind us, on a perfect afternoon. Not a tree in sight! Mike was having a field day with his camera.

Driving off we found that there was no longer any tarmac, just dirt. A very long queue of cars was waiting, hoping to cross before the ferry stopped for the day. I feared most of them would be stuck for the night.

The ferry across Lake Baikal to Olkhon.

Needing a pee, I proceeded to the public toilet block. My access was partially obstructed by a grazing cow, which showed no inclination to move aside. Finding that there was a single 'squat and grunt' cubicle was hardly a surprise, nor that it stank to high heaven. Out in the wilds mains drainage and a sewerage system may be uneconomic or impractical, but hadn't they heard of cesspits?

The road to Khuzhir was through an almost empty landscape. The coastline on the far side of the lake consisted of low cliffs falling more or less straight down into the water, not unlike some of the fjord country in North Norway.

The homestead where we were staying was a complex of wooden buildings decorated outside with woodcuts and the odd antler or two. We had an entrance lobby with a table and chairs and a shower and toilet, which as the occupants of Room A we obviously shared with those renting Room B. There was a large padlock on the door and we were issued with a key each. Only a small round table inside, so if Mike wanted that for his laptop while he edited his pictures then it was just as well there was another table in the lobby that I could use when writing up my journal.

During our stay, the dinner menu remained extremely limited: a starter of salad and omul* (a small white fish found only in Lake Baikal), followed by stewed chicken and mash or stewed beef and rice – there was no choice, it was on the menu and they alternated. Dessert was a sweetened bun which they put on the plate with your starter and if you were not careful you ate it with the salad and buggered up the flavours as they didn't match.

Our homestead.

The next morning, we had booked a tour of the island in a minibus, and were joined by two young French backpackers who didn't seem keen on talking to us until we sat down for lunch and I addressed them in French. We headed out of the village. There was no road as you and I would understand the term. Just dirt, no pavement for pedestrians, no kerb or kerbstones and so wide – 60m in fact, widening to 80m for the main north-south through road – that standing at the crossroads in the village centre the scene looked like something out a Western. I half expected to see Wells Fargo hurtling towards me in a cloud of Apache arrows and John Wayne riding shotgun.

We were soon well clear of the village. The land was once again very barren and wide open with clear views of the lake and the far shore and for mile after mile no signs of habitation. At the bottom of the slope were some tempting beaches. Olga said she came here every summer with her family from her home in Irkutsk*, 300km distant, to camp out for 'seaside' holidays. At this beach, the water is the shallowest in the lake, and therefore the warmest for swimming.

The road so far had been pretty bumpy. It was just a rutted track – or a choice of tracks across open country where you chose whether to go to the right where the ruts were half a metre deep or to the left where they were only two feet. In other words, they were appalling whichever way you went.

Olga said we'd seen nothing yet – in the forest they were even worse!

We didn't think that was possible. We were wrong. When we entered a small area of forest, we were tossed about like a roller-coaster ride even though we were in four-by-four vehicle. But our driver, Aleksei*, had been doing this trip on a more or less daily basis for visitors for the whole of the summer, and for who knows how many summers before. He knew which side of each rut to steer, even though in the back us passengers were bouncing about without seat-belts and without any hand grips to hold on to.

We reached the northern tip of the island, Cape Khoboi*. Aleksei dropped us off at a parking area close by, and told us to walk the rest of the way while he went off into the pinewoods to prepare our picnic lunch. The lake was flat calm, and this was also its widest point, just short of fifty miles (79.5kms).

By the time we returned to the van Aleksei had a fire going, a cauldron was simmering on a tripod and the scene was set for Act 4 Scene 1 of Macbeth ('Bubble, bubble' etc. etc.). A fixed table was laid for six with plates, cutlery, bread, tomatoes and salads to go with his soup of potatoes and omul.

Without warning we found we had an extra guest! A striking and fearless bird arrived to help himself only inches away from my elbow.

Our picnic lunches.

"What's he called?" I asked Aleksei and Olga.

"A sinitsa."* (which translates as 'blue and small')

I later discovered he was a rock nuthatch. He was obviously used to picnickers and the food they brought, and knew that they wouldn't do him any harm. Which was just as well, as he was perched on my plate while I was eating off it!

I learned pretty quickly how to eat boiled fish and potatoes with a spoon, as we had neither knives nor forks. Second helpings were followed by black tea poured from a kettle (but with sugar available). Dessert was another of those damned sweet buns.

We reached Cape Shunte* – 'Cape Left' – which is heart-shaped, and were regaled with a Buryat* legend. The Buryats are the indigenous people in this part of Siberia.

A childless couple wanting a child should sleep for three nights on the rock. If they want a boy then sleep on the right side of the rock, if a girl then on the left. Sleep in the middle if they want twins. If after a year they still remain childless the man should throw the woman into the lake.

Ah! – 'the good old days'!

After lunch off to Uzuri*, the only settlement on the island's east coast, which Olga told us has a meteorological station and a resident population of fifteen. There was a pond just inland behind a shingle beach and a few wandering cattle – and it was two hours by heavily rutted track to anywhere else. One wondered what the people who live here did to pass the time, living on a bare hillside looking out onto the lake. No matter how splendid the view, one couldn't spend all one's waking hours gazing at it. Or maybe they…?

Our day clocked up 100km, most of it over bone-shattering rutted tracks across barren, open country or through pine forest where there were transverse ruts a foot deep crossing the others. Were it not for our minibus having good springs and good upholstery, we'd have been black and blue.

Back in our room, Mike set about photographing the interior for posterity. There was a bucket of cold water and a large ladle, enabling you to fill the electric water heater above the sink. To plug the boiler in you had to disconnect the light as there was only one socket, so while the water was heating up you had no light in that part of the room. There was a liquid soap dispenser on the wall which was easy to find even in the dark – just look for the shiny icicle of spillage stuck to the wall underneath and follow it back to its source. I felt glad I'd brought my own soap. There was a notice in English asking guests not to waste water, yet there was no plug in the sink. You therefore had no option but to wash under a running tap as there was only the one. It was essential you didn't heat the water in the heater too much and scald yourself as you couldn't add cold water to lower the temperature.

There were two beds, but no bedside stand between them on which one could put anything, such as my watch and my glasses. We put one of our cases there as a substitute. There were no cupboards nor any bedside lights, just the one main light suspended in the middle of the room. The only switch for that was by the door, so you had to turn the light off before getting into bed and grope your way back in the dark (oops! sorry, Mike!).

Going for a pee during the night would entail finding one's way to the door in the dark, unlocking it, feeling one's way to the access door to the shower and toilet because that's where the switch is, turning on the light and then in reverse turning off the light and making one's way back, locking the door in the dark and stumbling back to one's bed. Who said the Friends of Nocturnal Diuresis would always be a misunderstood minority?

On the last morning I risked the shower, which functioned once you'd worked out which way to turn the tap to control the water temperature. I then walked down to the post office, where the only other customer was a short Buryat woman talking on her mobile phone while collecting her pension. As well as being clearly more plugged in to modern life than I am (I haven't got a mobile phone), she was wearing perfectly ordinary 'European' clothes. Ordinary Buryats don't wear traditional costume any more, but dress just like the rest of us.

I returned to collect Mike, who had taken a shower once I'd finished, and together we walked back into the village centre for him to take some souvenir photos of Khuzhir. We walked past a burnt-out minibus lying on its roof by the roadside and an abandoned car parked against someone's fence. In the middle of a crossroads lay a huge stagnant pond covered in algae and full of junk.

There were piles of logs outside garden gates and a water tanker was delivering to domestic premises. All over the place were plastic bags and bits of sheeting, flattened drink cans, broken glass, single discarded flip-flops, old tyres and general detritus. It gave the whole village an air of being thoroughly unloved. No one cared, or maybe they used to but they'd given up and were now past caring. If anyone dropped anything it looked as though they just walked on and the next passing vehicle squashed it flat and it became part of the scenery.

Whatever happened to civic pride?

It was eleven o'clock in the morning on a fine day, yet there was almost no one about and when we passed the school there was no sign of any children. Anyone notice a Pied Piper?

There was so little traffic you could wander at will all over the road, which was so rutted no one could drive at more than about 10mph and so wide that they could just drive around you. It made me wonder yet again why they had a sign on a post indicating a pedestrian crossing where nothing is painted on the road surface because there is no road surface. There was enough civic pride to want a pedestrian crossing sign in the middle of their village, but not enough to employ a bloke with a long-handled litter-picker to collect all the rubbish and dispose of it.

Our visit was now complete and it was time to go. I thought to myself, *I'll never be here again, and while I've enjoyed exploring Olkhon we've seen all there is to see. It may look different in winter when the lake is frozen.*

The 37km drive back to the ferry took an hour, bouncing about in places where the gravel and large stones gave way to bare earth and the ubiquitous ruts. We passed just one small settlement of half-a-dozen houses and a couple of isolated farms.

There were a few cars ahead of us in the queue. The small ferry was standing idle, but the crew refused to let anyone on until departure time.

This time the larger ferry was operational, returning with a load of cars, but once it had disgorged its cargo it, too, shut down. Presumably until the skipper looked at his watch and decided that his next timetabled crossing was now imminent.

We ended up waiting half an hour, time enough for a leisurely coffee on a veranda overlooking the strait and to make use of the café's facilities. I wasn't risking life and limb going anywhere near those public bogs again or having to squeeze past that cow.

Crossing again took fifteen minutes, with more wonderful photo-ops in all directions from our vantage point twenty feet above the car deck. We had indeed been fortunate with the weather – three weeks in Siberia almost without rain and the sun always shining, giving Mike ideal conditions to take photos.

It was goodbye to Olkhon, 'the island in the lake'. And to you, dear reader.

September 2012

Guide to Pronunciation

Aleksei:	*Alec-**syay***
Baikal:	*Buy-**kahl***
Buryat:	***Boo**-r-yat*
Irkutsk:	*Ear-**kootsk***
Khoboy:	*Hub-**boy***
Khuzhir:	*Hoo-**zheer***
Olga:	***Oil**-ga*
Olkhon:	*Oil-**khon***
omul:	***omm**-ool*
Shunte:	***Shoon**-the*
sinitsa:	*see-**nee**-tsa*
Uzuri:	*Oo-**zoo**-ree*

[*Adapted from 'Jottings from the Trans-Siberian Railway'. Other books are listed inside the front cover.*]

Postscript

Q: What is the first thing a ball does when it stops rolling?
A: It looks round.

Goodnight.

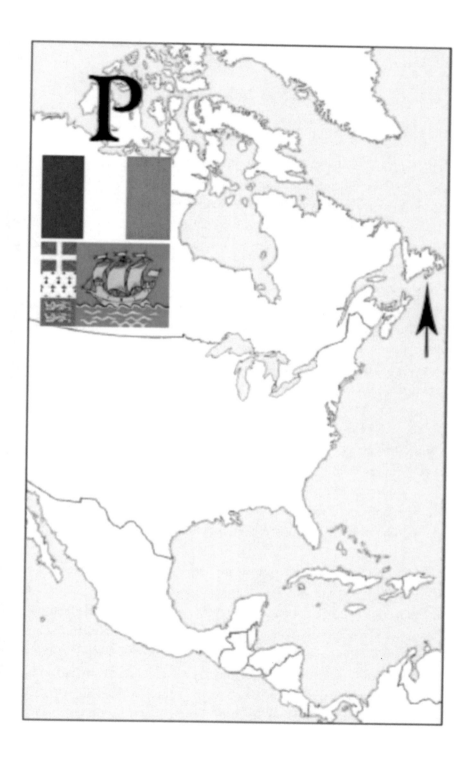

St Pierre & Miquelon
I Cod You Not!

"If you don't invite me soon," I wrote to my cousin Chris who lives in Nova Scotia, "I'll be too old and decrepit to come."

"Come next year," he replied. "Three weeks be enough?"

"If you can put up with me for that long under your feet. But it's a long way and I won't be doing it again, so maybe you're right that we allow time for me to see as much as I can."

Chris trained as a speech therapist. Recently married, he had been browsing a journal and saw a post advertised at a rehabilitation hospital in Edmonton, Alberta, and suggested to his wife, Renate, that they might go to Canada for a couple of years. Almost half a century later, they're still there. On retirement, they moved to Halifax to be nearer their daughter, Petra, and her family. They made periodic visits to England to see family and friends, and to Germany while Renate's parents were alive. We'd therefore met a few times over the years, as well as keeping in touch at birthdays and Christmas and exchanging emails.

"While I'm there," I added, "I want to go to St Pierre & Miquelon."

"We've never been!"

"Now's your chance. I'll never be anywhere near them again, and it fits in with my project to visit all the islands off the French coast. What's more, you live in Halifax which will have regular flights. You make the arrangements. I suggest four days."

I had to make a very early start as my departure time from Heathrow was 09h30 and, as everyone knows, you are expected to check in two hours beforehand. My friend Stuart had arranged to collect me at 03h15 and take me to Winchester to catch the coach, and arrived – fortunately – a quarter of an hour early to find me still in bed. My alarm had failed to go off! Luckily, I'd already packed, and it was a question of wiping my face, collecting my breakfast packet from the fridge and heading for the coach pick-up point by the King Alfred statue at the bottom of Winchester High St.

The flight itself was uneventful. On arrival Chris and Renate were waiting for me with their car. Although their postal address is Halifax, in fact their house is about twenty miles out of town. They settled me in, and the following day we set off back to the airport, this time to catch the plane to St Pierre on the local airline, imaginatively titled 'Air St Pierre'. Well, at least it rhymes.

Once on board the plane, the hostess explained the safety regulations in French and sat down.

"Notice something?" I whispered to Chris.

"What?"

"She's not going to repeat it in English. The attitude is: 'You're going to France, so you speak French! If not – tough'."

At the airport, this was made evident again, as my passport was handed back without being stamped. The UK is part of the EU, so is France, St Pierre & Miquelon are part of France. To pass from one EU country into another you only need ID. A UK passport doubles as ID, ergo your passport doesn't need to be stamped.

Chris and Renate had Canadian passports, which were duly stamped.

For most of the eighteenth century Britain and France were locked in a protracted struggle to claim and settle North America, but by the Treaty of Paris in 1763 all France's lands in Canada were ceded to Britain and in exchange they were awarded St Pierre & Miquelon. The islands changed hands yet again several times thereafter, usually with the population being expelled, but the islands were ultimately captured by Britain during the Napoleonic Wars. When the Bourbon dynasty was restored to the French throne, Louis XVIII successfully negotiated their return and they reverted to French rule in 1816.

These are two tiny, bleak and barren islands, often fog-bound in winter. Why were they considered worth putting up a fight to retain?

The answer is one word: cod.

Under the terms of the restoration, a sea area off St Pierre was designated as French territorial waters, which enabled them to establish a thriving fishing industry.

Cod fishing off the Grand Banks began at the end of the fifteenth century when, sailing in the service of King Henry VII, the Genoese explorer John Cabot discovered Newfoundland and claimed it for the English crown. The industry grew in importance and dominated the economies of the coastal towns and villages all around the St Lawrence estuary, especially in Newfoundland and Nova Scotia. However, in the 1990s it was discovered that the cod had been fished almost to extinction and the industry collapsed with the loss of 40,000 jobs.

In the heyday of the fishing industry in the 19th and 20th centuries conditions were harsh. St Pierre's museum exhibits testify to that reality. Two men worked a tiny fishing boat called a dory in all weathers, hauling cod inboard and then returning to the mother ship to unload. As they often worked out of sight of this vessel there are many sad stories of dorymen being lost at sea because they were unable to find their mother ship due to fog or bad weather, and others who were lost due to an Atlantic gale or when the mother ship itself went down.

Another ever-present hazard in the days before lighthouses was Sable Island, a notorious sand bar 300kms south-east of Halifax upon which many ships were wrecked because it constantly shifted its shape due to the movements of ocean currents. It was known as 'the graveyard of the Atlantic'.

On return to St Pierre, the mother ship landed its fish, which then had to be dried. This work was labour-intensive, as each individual fish had to be laid out by hand on a bed of stones to dry in the wind, all taken in at night and the entire process repeated next day until the catch was dry enough to be salted and packed in barrels for export.

Most of these stone beds were on the Île aux Marins, a small island facing St Pierre, and they survive to this day because the island was abandoned in 1963. Many of the houses remain, kept in good repair by their owners who can spend leisure time there provided they have their own food, water and a generator. When we visited, we were shown the former schoolhouse and a small museum, which along with more likely exhibits illustrating fishing and seafaring in former days boasted a comprehensive display of the islands' stamps.

To meet the demand for labour, boys from poor families in Brittany, Normandy and the Basque country were shipped in. Life was hard, the work repetitive, the wages low and neither education nor social care were provided. Unsurprisingly, many of the boys as they grew older turned to drink.

The modern museum doesn't pull its punches. At the top of its list of morbid attractions they proudly display a guillotine, which was brought from Martinique in 1889 to execute a murderer and has remained on the island ever since. Other exhibits depicted the thriving trade in alcohol during the 1920s in the days of prohibition. Millions of gallons of whisky were imported from Canada, not for local consumption but to be smuggled into the United States.

Once we had checked into our hotel, we went outside and hailed a taxi for a quick tour. The island of St Pierre is only 10sqm (26km/sq.), a more or less circular rock, and what little level land there is is of poor quality and unsuitable for agriculture. In any case, the climate is too harsh. The land slopes down to the sea on the south-eastern side and flattens out enough for a town and harbour to be built. Nine-tenths of the population of the islands live in this one spot.

Our driver pointed out various buildings as we passed them, such as the cathedral, the town hall and numerous restaurants. He then took us up the steep road behind the town to a viewpoint on the far side on the highest accessible point where we could see the harbour, the Île aux Marins and the airport.

Traditionally, St Pierre's clapboard houses were painted in bright colours. Plastic strips, designed to look like the original but more durable, have replaced wood.

The following day we joined a tourist boat to Miquelon, which is a village on the northern tip of an island of the same name, attached by a six-mile sandy isthmus to another island, Langlade, which is uninhabited, covered in forest and popular with local residents for hunting. Except where it joins the isthmus, on all sides cliffs plunge into the sea from a height of two or three hundred feet.

A few natural coves have summer residences accessible only by water, belonging to people with a private yacht. We admired them from a distance, as our boat took us up from the harbour in St Pierre to a landing point halfway along the aforesaid isthmus.

We stopped fifty yards off shore and a Zodiac inflatable boat came out to meet us. Donning lifejackets, we were helped aboard and taken to the beach. Someone had had the foresight to lay out a length of boarding projecting into the sea, and we managed to scramble out of the Zodiac onto the slats without getting our feet wet. At the top of the beach our local guide, Rita, was waiting for us with her car.

The cliffs of Langlade.

As we drove the length of the narrow isthmus towards Miquelon Rita explained how in the past it had been a hazard to shipping because of the frequent winter fog. It was low-lying and treeless and therefore difficult to see, and as no one lived on it there were no lights. One of the first things she showed us once we reached the village (pop 710) was a tombstone in the cemetery marking the last resting place of a British coxswain whose ship ran aground and was wrecked in 1874.

In Miquelon, the houses seemed to be well maintained, and there was a small harbour servicing the regular passenger ferries to St Pierre and to Newfoundland, which is some 15 miles distant and could just be seen on the horizon. We were amazed at the church – enormous, with room for the entire population!

Another local landmark was a memorial to Sister Hilarion, a nun who spent over 50 years in this backwater of the French colonial empire helping the poor and their children until her death in 2003.

"Lunch," said Rita, breezily. "There's a restaurant here (we were standing outside it), one over there (she pointed across the road) and another just down the street. I'll see you in an hour."

She walked away, presumably to go home. We looked at each other.

"What now?"

"Well, we're standing outside one. Why don't we go in and see what's what? If we don't fancy it, we can go to one of the others."

To my total amazement the menu offered a full range of starters, including escargots, and galettes and crêpes as main courses.

"Galettes – here!" I exclaimed in disbelief. "In France, you only get them on the menu in Brittany. Cross the border into Normandy and they shake their heads."

I couldn't believe my luck. In this back of beyond I was being offered one of my favourite dishes – and for good measure, a snails starter!

My biggest surprise in St Pierre & Miquelon has to be having a lunch of escargots followed by a galette forestière in an isolated village at the very end of the road to nowhere. We were also highly amused by the alacrity with which, the moment we'd left, the proprietors closed the door gently but firmly behind us and turned around the 'Ouvert' sign in the window to read 'Fermé'.

Even in such a far-flung outpost, French cuisine maintained normal service!

After all, at half past two and with no passing trade, what was the point of staying open?

July 2015

Postscript

At the very outset, their marriage was blissfully happy.
But on the way to the vestry…

Goodnight.

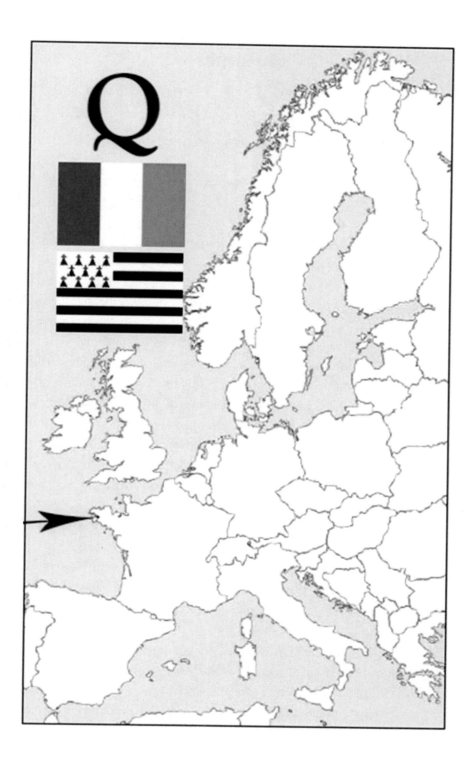

Q

Quimper
A Scheduled Trip Becomes Two

[Conversations in italics were in French]

Located in the far south-west of Brittany, Quimper lies at the junction of two rivers, the Steir and the Odet. Anyone with even a modicum of French knows that it's pronounced 'Cam-pair', with the stress on the second syllable. Adrian, my younger half-brother and a determined monoglot, insisted on pronouncing it 'Quim-purr', with heavy stress on the first syllable and refused outright to say it in the French manner. With his wife Myrtle completing the party, he was doing the driving in return for me showing them around Brittany and doing the talking. To no avail, I pointed out that should he ask directions, the response from a local about the way to 'Quim-purr' would be the proverbial Gallic shrug.

Quimper is best known for its faience pottery museum and as the birthplace of René Laennec, who in 1816 invented the stethoscope when, so it is alleged, he felt embarrassed at having to put his ear directly onto ladies' chests to hear their heartbeat, and devised a hollow wooden tube to save his blushes.

The Odet, the Bretons claim, is their prettiest river and in summer it is possible to take a boat ride downstream to Benodet, where it enters the sea. The town centre in Quimper is intersected by bridges over the rivers, which give it a most interesting town centre to explore on foot.

I'd visited before with Margaret, and had a nasty experience when I left the car in an underground car park and when it came to paying the charge and getting out, I couldn't understand the instructions. Fortunately, a local lady retrieving her own vehicle saw me having trouble and kindly came to my rescue by showing me how the system worked. I resolved that if I ever came to Quimper again – as I did – I would park in the open air!

Benodet, on the coast, boasts fine beaches but the reason we were there was that in summer, boats from the little harbour take tourists on day trips to the Glénan Islands. We'd booked a flat for the week and set out next morning for our day trip – only to find that the season had ended the weekend before and we were one week too late! Bugger! Why didn't I check? We'd have to come back another year, at least a week earlier.

Faience plate.

All was not lost. There were lots of pretty villages and small towns, particularly along the coast, worth a brief visit to walk around, take a few photos and pop into a restaurant for some local cuisine. And there was, of course, Quimper itself, the capital of the region and in many people's opinion the capital of Breton culture. Farther east lay Concarneau, famous for its *ville close* or walled town, the impregnable fortifications begun in the fourteenth century to defend the harbour. Entrance was across a bridge and through a fortified gateway. Inside the walls the main street was thronged with visitors enjoying the cafés, restaurants and souvenir shops. Up side streets it was possible to see how the fortifications functioned in their heyday. We had the good luck to discover a small café tucked away from the main street and offering the exhausted visitor the opportunity to have a rest and enjoy some refreshment *al fresco*.

Concarneau's 'ville close' encircled by ramparts and dominated by a belfry.

Beyond Concarneau lay Pont Aven, famous as the home of artists of the 'Pont Aven School' which flourished after a short but influential stay by Paul Gaugin in 1886. It's a picturesque enough village to enjoy on foot, but our experience was marred by the dismissive treatment by the *maitre d'hotel* at a restaurant we chose, who shunted us into a corner and thrust his English language menu into our hands without bothering to enquire if that was what we wanted. In France, I always opt for the French menu because I often have trouble trying to decrypt the English version where the dishes have been translated by a chef who doesn't know any English and concocts it using a dictionary.

To add to our discomfiture, there was a large party of locals at a long table making a lot of noise, we presumed someone's office party celebrating their promotion, forthcoming marriage or similar. Whatever the reason for their gaiety, they were so inconsiderate of other diners by virtue of their shouting and uninhibited laughter that we left the menus on the table and walked out. We found a café on the outskirts of the village, replete with square tables covered with plastic tablecloths with a chequered pattern and had a perfectly acceptable meal in unpretentious surroundings.

Rather more enjoyable was a visit in the other direction, westwards, where without any preconceived expectations we lit upon Pont-l'Abbé. Parking just over the bridge, we explored what there was of the town, then found a table in a restaurant in a prominent corner position bursting at the seams. We soon found out why: they had an excellent and varied menu and their seafood was delicious.

We rented the same flat in Benodet the following year, having of course checked that we were 'in season' so far as boat trips out to the Îles de Glénan were concerned. The archipelago lies ten miles out to sea and consists of a roughly circular ring of ten islands and a handful of islets creating a lagoon which the locals call La Chambre ('the room'). On the main island, St Nicholas, there's a restaurant, a bar, a few cottages available for rent in the season and an internationally renowned diving school. None of the other islands are any longer inhabited. Diving or sailing are the sole remaining economic activities, along with catering for day trippers in the summer.

Glenan Islands boardwalk.

Rather than go direct, the boat meandered close to several islands so that the guide, sitting in the front with a microphone and delivering his narrative entirely in French, could tell us something about them. The land mass of tiny Île Cigogne is almost entirely covered by an enormous fort, originally built in the 18th century to prevent the islands being occupied by British or Dutch pirates and modernised and expanded later. Penfret Island is dominated by its lighthouse, now of course automated, but where in the 1920s, our guide told us, the lighthouse keeper and his wife had eleven children. My guess was that confined to a rocky island only ten acres square, there wasn't much else to do…

We didn't require much time on Île St Nicholas to walk around and admire the views, and enjoyed lunch in the open air before embarking for the return trip. The islands are renowned for their pristine white sand beaches. The colour and clarity of the water in La Chambre explains why diving has been taught there for half a century. On our return trip, the boat took a different route, giving the guide the opportunity to extol the virtues of other islands and islets and regale us with stories about shipwrecks.

In the late nineteenth century the total population scattered on the islands was sufficient in number to maintain a school and have the services of a full-time priest. It seems that the islands supported a comparatively large population right up to the mid-twentieth century, growing potatoes and wheat or being otherwise employed in fishing, particularly shellfish, harvesting seaweed, maintaining the fort and ensuring that the lighthouses kept functioning around the clock to preserve safety at sea. All, sadly, have now departed.

Since 1974 the islands have been managed as France's smallest nature reserve, a decision which saved from probable extinction the unique Glénan narcissus, which in April covers the islands in an off-white carpet. It grows in short grass and when the population left and farming was abandoned the land reverted to scrub and this indigenous flower was in real danger of dying out.

No building is now permitted anywhere on the islands, although two remain in private hands. Nowadays the permanent population drops in winter to four, presumably maintenance staff to monitor any damage caused by Atlantic gales and make any necessary repairs.

Abbaye de Landévennec.

Back on the mainland, our farthest excursion took us up to the north coast of the Crozon peninsula to the ruins of the Abbaye de Landévennec, where the medicinal and herb gardens have been restored to how they would have appeared in Charlemagne's time (c. 800AD) although monks first occupied the site in the sixth century. The sheer scale of the ruins gives an idea of how rich the church was in the Middle Ages.

On the wall behind the souvenir stall I noticed a photo which I thought I recognised.

"Is that Skellig Michael?"

The assistant, visibly shaken, replied, *"Er, yes."* He was clearly surprised that a casual visitor recognised the photo.

"Have you been there, then?"

"Er, no. We think some of the monks from here went there at some point, or perhaps it was a daughter house."

"We went there a few years ago. It's 12kms out in the Atlantic off the south-west coast of Ireland and must have been the most isolated monastery in Europe."

As you have probably noted, this corner of Brittany is less frenetic than those parts more fancied by holidaymakers, as anyone who's ever attempted to thrust and squirm their way up to the top of Mont St Michel will confirm, or tried to find a table in a restaurant on Belle Île at the height of the season. Yet even though we had to come two years running in order to get to the Glénans we still found enough of interest to gently pass the time.

If some of the places we found ourselves in by sheer chance were not sufficiently interesting to feature in this tale there were others which were, and perhaps having read about them here new visitors will follow in our footsteps. But if you want to follow in our footsteps to the Îles de Glénan, remember to check the ferry schedules before you go!

October 2008, September 2009 and July 2012

Postscript

First man: "In my opinion, there's nothing more disgusting than picking your nose in public and eating it."

Second man: "Yes, there is."

First man: "What's that, then?"

Second man: "Picking someone else's nose and…"

Bon voyage – and *goodnight!*

R

RIGA

Blackheads and Black Balsam

Mike and I were in Latvia at the start of a planned visit across three of the Baltic States, intending to proceed to Lithuania and Finland in the course of the next three weeks. We'd been collected at the airport and brought to Hotel Mercure and Reception had pointed us in the direction of the lift to Room 418. We'd settled in and sorted out, as was almost second nature on our travels, who'd have which bed and which shelves and had divided available wardrobe space as we'd be here for four nights and therefore would unpack everything and stow it away. Both being on permanent age-related medication, we also regularly checked with each other that we'd taken it.

"Dinner?"

"Not half. We've had nothing to eat since breakfast."

We sat down directly in front of the chef, who was cooking on a hob while demonstrating remarkable skills as a juggler. On his belt, he carried a sheath for his slicing knife. Every time he used it he wiped it on a cloth and then tossed it full circle and caught it safely by the handle, then thrust it back into the sheath without looking. His nonchalance indicated his absolute confidence that he wouldn't miss and stab himself in the midriff.

The best part of his act was still to come. Using a sort of turner, he proceeded to toss an egg in the air from one side to the other, then catching it on the edge, picking it off with his other hand and cracking it on the hob. A little later he attracted attention by igniting the oil to create a two-metre-high fireball. To while away the time between preparing dishes he juggled with the turner and his two-pronged fork. While I was engrossed in watching his performance, the food on my plate went cold!

By ten o'clock we'd finished eating, but although it seemed rather early to go to bed, we'd been up since the early hours and had had a pretty exhausting day getting to Heathrow and then landing in Helsinki late and having to change planes at the double. On the morrow, we had a guide booked to show us the highlights of the Riga's historic centre, so maybe an early night would be a sensible idea.

We entered the Old Town through the Swedish Gate, an archway cut through the city walls in 1698 when after a prolonged siege by the Russians the Swedish garrison finally surrendered because of famine. Peter the Great was so impressed by their bravery that he allowed them to leave with honour, still carrying their weapons. The Gate survived, but Riga has suffered a lot of destruction in wars, starting with the French in 1812, then WW1 and the struggle for independence from Tsarist Russia, followed by WW2 and invasion by the Soviet Union, then by the Nazis, then by the Soviet Union again.

In the archway of the Swedish Gate a lady of middling years with very long, dyed blond, hair was busking on a kokle*, a native Latvian instrument shaped rather like a zither. It produces a remarkably soothing sound.

We ended up in the main square, facing the restored House of the Blackheads. In the Middle Ages this was the name of a guild of young, unmarried German merchants and sea captains. It was hugely influential, as a place where deals were made and letters of introduction or credit were exchanged. There were similar 'Houses' in other Hansa towns. The guild adopted as their patron saint St Maurice, a Roman legionary commander who was martyred for his Christian faith in 287AD. He was reputed to have come from Upper Egypt and the early Church depicted him as a black man in full armour – hence the guild's name. The original building was completely destroyed in WW2, but after regaining their independence the Latvians wanted their history back and built a replica.

At this point Anita, our guide, left us to find some lunch and our own way back to the hotel. A nearby restaurant had a display board featuring local cuisine. When we chose onion soup it came in a round loaf of bread hollowed out with the top sliced off to form a detached 'lid', with a crusty knob to serve as a handle.

The House of the Blackheads.

It was so filling that I couldn't eat anything more.

The menu also featured a local drink, 'black balsam'.

"Sounds like something you sniff up your nose over a hot bowl when you've got a cold," I ventured.

"That's friar's balsam," said Mike. "I'll ask the waitress. Can we have some?"

"It's not the sort of drink you have with a meal," the waitress replied, in casual English. "It's a digestive, not an aperitif."

We decided to try it, and were pleasantly surprised. Further enquiries revealed that it is a traditional Latvian infusion of plants and has been made in Riga since the middle of the eighteenth century, and is reputed to have medicinal properties.

The next day we drove to Rundale* to see the eighteenth century palace designed for the Duke of Courland by Rastrelli, the renowned architect who designed The Hermitage in St Petersburg.

Anita explained: "The palace was largely abandoned when the next duke moved to Berlin and emptied Rundale to furnish his new palace. When Napoleon invaded Russia in 1812, Rundale was used as a hospital. It became a school in the mid-nineteenth century and then suffered further damage during our struggle for independence in 1918. During the period of Soviet occupation, it was used as a storehouse. Only since we regained our independence in 1990 has the restoration of the palace to its former glory begun."

The achievements so far were, nonetheless, very impressive. Because of the general lack of furniture, one's gaze focused on the restored stucco work on the walls and the wonderfully repainted ceilings.

Note the two ceramic stoves on either side of the alcove.

Very little of the original furniture had survived, having been either removed or looted. What was there consisted mostly of chairs, bought at auction and then placed in the palace. They were authentic for the period, but were not the original items that were here in the palace's heyday in the late eighteenth century.

For dinner, we fancied a change so set off into town. We discovered an alleyway which opened out to create an enclosed courtyard of cafés and restaurants, open to the skies but totally surrounded by tall apartments and hence protected from the elements. For the comfort of customers who preferred to sit outside, especially those who wanted to smoke while enjoying coffee or a glass of wine, the restaurants supplied blankets. The staff folded them over each chair and when clients finished their meal, they left the blanket on the chair for the next customer.

"That seems to me to be a very civilised practice," I remarked to Mike.

"It works," he replied, "because the customers don't spill things on the blankets or otherwise mess them up, and don't walk off with them. It's based on trust."

Back in the hotel our thoughts turned to organising a smooth departure. To be sure of getting to the bus station in good time, we decided to walk there before dinner to spy out the land. The public service bus left too early for us to have lunch prior to departure. By the time we arrived at our destination, Klaipeda* in Lithuania, it would be too late.

We would need to buy some food and drink for the journey. Luckily there were two shopping malls on the way, and we found a kiosk selling sandwiches, drinks, newspapers and magazines.

"We'll have no problem tomorrow morning provisioning ourselves for the bus journey," Mike observed with satisfaction.

"Yes," I said. "We have to pass the entrance, and we'll be able to make a bee-line for the shop because we now know exactly where it is."

What we couldn't find were any newspapers in English, which I thought rather surprising in a capital city where the educated young all learn it.

"Here's something," I said. "It's called The Baltic Times."

It was a 24-page monthly broadsheet in English featuring in-depth articles on political and cultural events in all three Baltic countries. It would be interesting to read about what was going on in the country, Latvia, we were currently visiting, the country, Lithuania, where we were headed tomorrow and the country, Estonia, which we'd spent time in the previous year.

For our last night in Riga we walked into the centre, checking out restaurants as we went and finally choosing a rather up-market one which offered interesting food and quiet background music.

After finishing the meal, I wanted to enjoy a cigar. When we went outside to take our coffee sitting at one of their pavement tables, a waiter thoughtfully put an overhead heater on just for us and brought us two blankets each. The heater may be environmentally questionable, but what the hell! It's always very pleasant to sit outside in the warm and people-watch over coffee and a cigar in any location. That I was doing so in a mildly exotic one, the centre of Riga, gave the experience an extra bounce.

Mike had been rather taken by that local speciality, black balsam, and we had the good fortune to pass a liquor store selling a wide range of alcoholic drinks. Assorted bottles, including black balsam, were displayed in the shop window.

"Have you got the sort with blackcurrant flavour?" Mike asked the assistant.

"Of course, sir," came the reply, in well-practised English.

"Now you've got what you want, I think I'd better get some, too," I said. "I don't want to leave Latvia without some local specialities. I don't care for black balsam myself, but a bottle will make a suitably exotic Christmas present for one of my friends with discerning taste buds."

Time had come to leave, and we spent a quiet morning packing. Thanks to last night's practice run, we knew how long it would take us with our luggage to get to the bus depot and we could organise our departure without haste.

We gave ourselves an hour between leaving the hotel and getting on the bus. That way we wouldn't have to hurry through busy streets pulling our cases or worry if there was a queue when buying our food and drink for the journey.

At the bus station the departure boards showed that the network was remarkably extensive, with buses for Moscow, St Petersburg, Minsk and Budapest, among others. Even, of all places, to Stuttgart. People in Riga want a direct bus to Stuttgart? In comparison with such far-flung destinations, our four-hour ride to Klaipeda was almost a local service, albeit starting in one country and ending in another.

We left a minute early, but spent three-quarters of an hour making detours to the ferry terminal and then out to the airport. We may have left the bus station at a quarter past twelve, but we didn't leave Riga until one o'clock.

Finally escaping the city, we drove through a succession of farms and pastures, then enormous fields of corn, then forested areas. Then the same again, only in a different order.

I'd been wondering what would happen at the border with Lithuania. The answer was: nothing! A roadside sign said 'Lietuva'*, the name of the country in Lithuanian, and we drove straight past it. The old road lay in a hollow on the right, now by-passed by the new straight road on which we were travelling. The former customs controls were still in place but abandoned and derelict. There were no longer any border crossing posts with officials to look at passports and stamp them.

Sadly, it's taken some of the fun out of being able to look up passport stamps and recall the circumstances when you got them. To get this frisson I have to riffle through all my old passports which provide permanent evidence of my travels around the continent in my student days in the 1950s.

Hey, ho!

September 2015

[Adapted from "Jottings from Russia and the Baltic States. Part 2: Latvia, Lithuania and Finland." Other books are listed inside the front cover.]

Guide to Pronunciation

Klaipeda:	**Kly**-*pedd-a*
kokle:	**cock**-*luh*
Lietuva:	*Lyet-oo-**va***
Rundale:	*Roon-**dahl**-a*

Postscript

Diarrhoea,
Twice a year,
Keeps you fit,
Keeps you clear.

Goodnight

Salou

Flags from the Past Foreshadow
Problems for the Future

In the early 1980s life was pretty hectic. I was teaching full-time, plus four classes a week after school at the local technical college. There I taught Russian to children who'd committed to come in from their own school at 4.15 for an hour-and-a-half's lesson twice a week for two years to get an extra O level. Margaret was teaching two-and-a-half days a week and most Mondays sitting as a magistrate. We were both on the borough council, where Margaret was Liberal Group Leader. Thinking about how she fancied a bit of a breather and some winter sunshine, she spotted an advert by a local coach company for a week in Spain coinciding with the October half-term break at a knock-down, inclusive price. I didn't need much persuading of the attractions of Salou, which lies on the Mediterranean coast some 70 miles south of Barcelona.

The journey itself should have been a warning that this holiday wasn't going to be all roses and padded armchairs... The coach started from the coach company's office ten miles distant in Bursledon, made various pick-ups and at Chandler's Ford we were almost the last to embark. The coach stopped briefly in Winchester, and then off to Dover for the ferry. So far, so good. But once in France, instead of breaking the journey with an overnight stay in a hotel, the drivers stopped at motorway restaurants at intervals to allow passengers to get a quick wash and brush-up and something to eat and once we were all safely back on board changed places and resumed driving. Sitting upright in a coach for nigh on 24 hours was not an experience either of us relished, but then if you pay bottom dollar you can't expect top dollar conditions. We arrived at our hotel exhausted and needing some serious sleep.

On the positive side, the hotel had its own small, private, sandy beach. Moreover, even at the end of October the sea temperature was warm enough for bathing. However, another feature of the knock-down price for the holiday was that the hotel restaurant operated two menus. One was for ordinary patrons the other a set menu for coach parties which meant that for a week we were fed hake every night unless we chose to pay extra for something different. It gave life to the phrase 'below the salt'. We felt that us package tourists were regarded by the management as a nuisance which they wished they could do without but as they needed our money, they tolerated us – just.

In Salou itself there was a memorial on the sea front honouring King Jaume ('Hoy-mee', or James) I of Aragon who set sail in 1229 to strike a blow against the Moorish pirates constantly raiding his coast. By conquering their base, Mallorca, he began the process by which during the Middle Ages Aragon dominated the western Mediterranean. He established an overseas empire which at times included Sicily and Naples (which in those days ruled the whole of southern Italy). We realised that the omnipresent red-and-yellow flag wasn't festival bunting but the Catalan provincial flag. On our return coach journey home, we noticed – as we hadn't on the way down – that it was also displayed on public buildings north of the Pyrenees. It wasn't flown just in Spain but also in France.

We also noticed something else we'd not perceived before, namely the appearance of the spelling 'Catalunya' which we twigged must be the way it was spelled in the local language. In recent years Spain has been wracked by political crises caused by the Catalan regional government's attempts to secede from Spain and Madrid's reaction, resulting in elections and changes of government. Looking back, the seeds of this conflict were even then apparent.

On later motoring holidays in this part of southern France, Roussillon, we learned that following the collapse of the Roman Empire the area had for long periods of its history been part of a country which bestrode the mountains, ruled successively by the Visigoths, the Vandals, the Moors, the counts of Barcelona and the kings of Aragon. The modern frontier between France and Spain only dates from 1659, when the Peace of the Pyrénées was signed between the two countries.

Our drivers put their coach at our disposal for a number of trips to places of interest. One was to the middle of Barcelona where they parked up and left us time to wander the length of La Rambla and back and find our own lunch. We were driven past the famous Sagrada Familia church designed by Antoni Gaudí and still unfinished a century after construction began. Our driver said it wasn't open to visitors. He then drove us to the former Olympic Stadium, which for some reason he thought worth seeing. It was empty and appeared dilapidated if not actually derelict, and we couldn't think why he'd bothered.

Construction of the Sagrada Familia began in 1882 and is still funded by private donations. Completion is forecast for 2026.

On another day, they took us into the mountains behind Barcelona to visit the basilica of the Benedictine monastery of Montserrat which houses the most famous shrine in Catalonia, the Black Madonna. Tradition says that it was carved in Jerusalem in biblical times but more probably it dates from the twelfth century. The reason the face of the Virgin is black is simply the effects of ageing.

The shrine is popular with coach parties, so our visit was crowded and we had to queue.

We'd read about the extensive Roman remains in Tarragona and took ourselves there by train. The city was probably founded by the Phoenicians in the fifth century BC and it seemed relatively relaxed and, shall one say, elegant, after the hustle and bustle of central Barcelona.

Remains of the Roman walls in Tarragona.

We had all day to explore the well-preserved relics of the Roman Empire, including amphitheatres and even stretches of the original defensive walls.

Our week's holiday was not particularly eventful, but with hindsight it had long-term consequences. Hitherto our focus for holidays had been in the main restricted to France and the Low Countries. It now broadened to include an interest in the Hispanic world. In the mid-1990s this resulted in us acquiring a time-share, not in Spain proper but in Lanzarote in the Canary Islands. Due to the change-over day being a Thursday we were unable to take this up while Margaret was still working. But in 2000 she, too, retired and we agreed that henceforward we'd go every year.

I remarked to her: "We're going to be spending a week or a fortnight in Lanzarote every year from now on for the rest of our lives, so I'd better learn the language." I devoted four years to weekly evening classes. Older readers having doubts about whether they would be able to cope with returning to study may feel encouraged when I tell them that at the age of 73 I passed AS level. This was sufficient, I thought, for my purposes which were purely practical, such as being able to read a bus timetable or ask someone for directions and understand the answer.

Fate, however, intervened and unexpectedly foreshortened 'the rest of our lives' to barely ten years. Margaret consulted her GP about the breathing difficulties she was experiencing when walking up a steep slope on the way to the shops and he sent her to hospital for what he assured her were routine tests. It took them exactly a fortnight to make an accurate diagnosis and commence treatment. Sadly, it was too late. That evening I came to visit with clean laundry and the day's paper. She was relieved to see me, but clearly in a distressed state. Within twenty minutes she lapsed into unconsciousness and died with me sitting beside her holding her hand.

Readers who have been widowed will know that one of the less acknowledged side effects of losing one's spouse or partner is that henceforth holidays present a problem because the person you habitually spent them with is no longer around. Dilemma: do you travel alone or find other companions? 'Mix and match' was my solution, but I have since disposed of the time-share. That decision carried with it an addendum: I no longer had any incentive to maintain my ability to speak Spanish.

On a visit to France some twenty years later Margaret and I stayed in Canet, near Perpignan. One day we decided to drive over the border into Spain as I had a few pesetas (the Spanish currency before the euro was introduced) and thought I might as well spend them. We were amused to pass what had formerly been the customs post between Cerbère in France and Port Bou in Spain. It was abandoned, with only the tricolour of France and the national coat of arms of Spain on either side of the entrance to indicate that inside this building the traveller moved from one country to the other and was required to present his passport to be stamped and possibly have his vehicle and baggage examined by customs officials. Not anymore!

Margaret at the abandoned frontier. post

Nowadays when travelling on the continent where most EU countries are members of the Schengen Area, we are accustomed to crossing national frontiers and scarcely being aware that we've done so because there are no checks. Back in the 1980s and the early years of this century it was a novel experience for an English traveller because our country's frontier with continental Europe is not land but sea and hence you can't pop across it without noticing.

It was on this visit to Roussillon that we drove alongside the remains of the *Via Domitia*, the original Roman road connecting Rome to Hispania (the Latin name for Spain), where it crossed the Pyrénées. It is still visible as a stony, overgrown track in a shallow valley despite two thousand years of wear and tear, not to mention the weather, before the modern road was constructed.

Strongholds such as Carcassonne and tiny Castelnou and the heavily fortified towns in the foothills of the mountains such as Prats-de-Mollo, Céret and St-Jean-Pla-de-Corts attest to the region being in the past hotly contested between rival kings or local warlords. But that is perhaps for another story which may also provide an opportunity to reveal the history and popularity of the Catalan national folk dance, the sardana.

October 1982

Postscript

People think that same-sex marriage is a new idea, but it's not. It existed in Scotland hundreds of years ago and was so prevalent on the islands off the west coast that they were called the Islands of the He-brides.

The monks writing the chronicles in the 6th and 7th centuries were scandalised by this, so they left out the hyphen, hoping no one would notice.

Goodnight.

T

ULAN BATOR

Terelj*

Alone on The Mongolian Steppe, Darkness Engulfed Me

Mike and I arrived on schedule in Ulan Bator*, the capital of Mongolia, at 06h10 and were last off the train as we'd mixed up the change of time-zone (again). Joey, our Mongolian guide, put us in his waiting taxi, and headed straight out of town north-east to our destination: Terelj National Park. It took 1¼ hrs over roads of ever-increasing undulation – potholes everywhere and our driver was forced to weave from side to side trying to avoid them, with varying degrees of success.

Once out of the capital the countryside became hilly and there were mountains on the horizon. The city's limits are extensive and one-third of Mongolia's population live in the capital, which they refer to as 'UB' for short. Once outside the sprawling city the land is virtually empty – as is, for that matter, most of Mongolia. It has a population of three million people in a country the size of Western Europe. Naturally, the road was not tarmac but simply earth, with no edge marked. The edge was where the last vehicle drove and left tyre marks, in the process widening the 'road'.

Our accommodation was at a country club which housed its guests in a traditional Mongolian ger*. This is a round tent made of white felt, about thirty feet in diameter with a central iron chimney stack. The nomadic herders who invented them would dismantle them when they moved on, loading everything onto carts and pack animals.

Our encampment was on a hillside with a picturesque view over a valley towards small forested areas and boasted several rows of gers. The only permanent buildings were the restaurant and the newly installed toilet block. There were five uneven concrete steps from the path up to the door of our ger which had a padlock (very traditional!). By the doorposts were gaps in the felt at ground level where the men who erected it hadn't done it properly. It didn't look too promising. I foresaw the wind whistling in at night when we were trying to (a) keep warm and (b) sleep. Once inside and alone, we found the door when closed didn't stay closed as the catch was broken. We had to find a piece of rope and create a makeshift loop so as to tie it shut.

According to tradition, inside a *ger* the left-hand side is the men's side, the right hand for women and children and there are no curtains or screens so there's no privacy. On each side was a large bed with a low headrest and drawers underneath or attached to the end of the bed to store clothing and bedding or, indeed, anything else. In the centre of the ger was the central supporting pole and the closed iron stove, absolutely essential in a country where in January the temperature can drop to -40°C. The chimney poked up through a hole in the roof and those putting our ger up had to make it watertight by wrapping additional felt around the stack. Also in the middle of the roof was a plastic transparent section which admitted daylight. Traditionally there was no natural light inside a ger once the door was shut.

Our beds were made up with pillows and duvets. There were three small stools and a table, meaning that we had nothing to sit on which supported our backs. Electricity from on-site generators reached each individual ger by an overhead cable supported by 3m-high metal poles positioned at intervals along the path, each with a lamp at the top. We had energy-saving bulbs dangling bare over our beds and another above the table, on which were a candle-end and some matches for emergencies. A young man came in with wood and lit the stove, which very soon threw out so much heat that it was actually too much and we had to open the door to reduce the temperature.

The weather was warm and sunny. I rummaged in my case and fished out some instant coffee. I sat smoking a small cigar while we enjoyed a bucolic view through our front door as it swung on its hinges emitting a grinding noise. The guide books had warned us that Mongolia had no oil.

The Club proprietors had realised that foreign tourists put much store in having Western standards of washing facilities and we were delighted to discover the WCs in the toilet block were a proper flush and not a 'squat and grunt'. The adjacent wash basins were unisex, communal and clean. There were four cubicles, but unfortunately in only one of them was there any toilet paper.

They'd also decided to provide Western-style food for breakfast: muesli, cornflakes and fried eggs – though ours had hard yolks and were served with a Frankfurter sausage sliced lengthways. They offered bread, butter and what looked like marmalade. It was a jam with a taste rather like apricot. Presumably a mixture of fruit, but quite palatable.

After lunch, we set off in the car with Joey along switch-back roads into the hills to see a Buddhist shrine. The landscape was reminiscent of the foothills of the Pyrénées or the Massif Central. That it was sub-alpine was not surprising when one considered that we were 1500m above sea level. On the way, we passed a few ponies and a solitary dromedary with their owners, waiting patiently for customers to stop their cars and buy a ride for their children. We pressed on.

The Buddhist temple was astounding, built at the top of a precipitous slope under the lee of mountain tops, and at even greater height above it multi-coloured inscriptions had been painted directly onto the rock face in positions where you cannot imagine how those who put them there did it other than abseiling off ropes from the summits. It was a long walk uphill, then up a couple of hundred steps to the shrine itself at a gradient of about 1:3. The view back down the valley from this vantage point was reward enough for the struggle to reach it.

That night I woke at 02h15 to the sound of rain falling onto the sloping roof just three feet above my head, as my bed was against the wall. I reached up to the light switch dangling loose just above my head and slipped on my shoes, anorak and cap intending to nip outside for a surreptitious pee.

Once I bent forward to put my shoes on I realised the floor was shining in the glare of the bare electric light bulb – the rain was coming in down the hole for the chimney stack. I was in no position to do anything about it and in any case, was being driven by a greater imperative – pressure in my bladder.

To get outside, I had to silently unloop the piece of rope holding the door shut in case a gust of wind blew it open. Outside, the lamps on their posts were all still switched on, despite the hour. I manoeuvred my way down the uneven steps with neither banister nor guard rail from our doorway to *terra firma* and walked around to the far side of the ger away from the toilet block, just in case there was anyone about. There I was, feet well apart to avoid pissing on my shoes, cap on my head to keep my hair and my glasses dry and wearing my anorak to keep the gentle rain off my naked body, in full flow (!) when – the lights fused! Although I was outside there was no light from the moon or stars because it was raining. It was absolutely pitch-black. I couldn't see the hand in front of my face, yet had to finish the business in hand because I couldn't stop. When I'd finished, somehow, I had to grope my way back up those uneven concrete steps, go inside, try to shut the door and loop the rope, hang my coat up in pitch darkness and wriggle out of my wet shoes and creep back into bed all without waking my ger-mate.

Not a chance! Mike was by now wide awake, and pissing himself with laughter. He was picturing my predicament outside. I was just glad he hadn't got flash and his camera handy. When I woke up again at 06h00, I found to my relief that the rain had stopped and the weather would be clear for our next excursion.

September 2012

[Adapted from 'Jottings from the Trans-Siberian Railway'. Other books are listed inside the front cover.]

Guide to Pronunciation

ger:	*grrr*
Terelj:	*Ter-**eldge***
Ulan Bator:	*Oo-**laan Baa**-tar*

Postscript

    The greatest player
in the football club's
history was a goalkeeper
named James Foot.
He was a leg-
end in his own lifetime.

Goodnight.

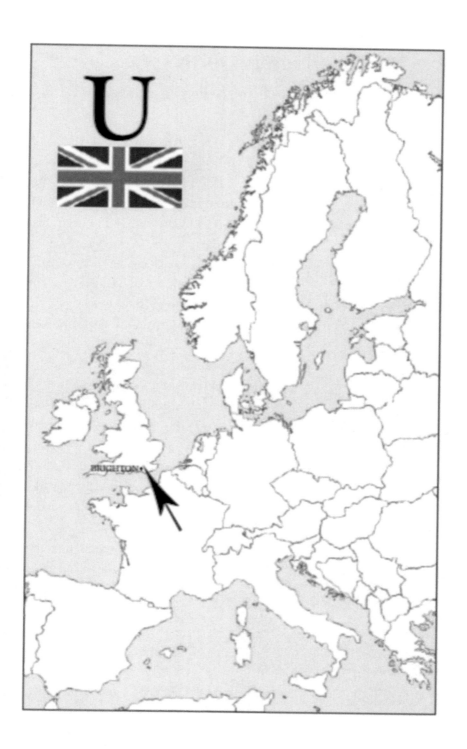

U

University of Sussex
Standing Up to Extremists

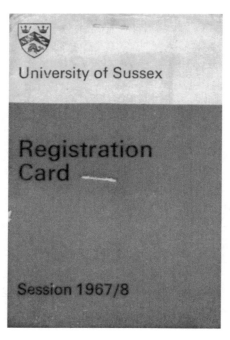

In 1967 I was seconded by my employer – Hampshire County Council – to enrol on an MA course in Russian Studies at Sussex University. I'd been teaching Russian to A level and had told them that as I only had A level in Russian myself I needed to acquire a higher qualification. They agreed.

During my time at the university I lodged at a special school for maladjusted children at Bolney, some eight miles north of Brighton, run by John Wallbridge, a friend from my undergraduate days at Southampton, my first university. He offered me bed and board during the week free of charge, saying that I'd be an extra pair of hands at night if there was an emergency, e.g. one of the children did a runner (not infrequent). I went home at weekends.

There were only three of us on the MA course, which required us to study

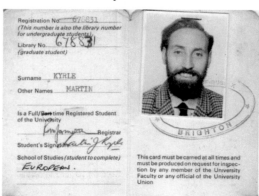

Russian history and literature but with an emphasis on the post-revolutionary Soviet period, a field with which I was totally unfamiliar. The A level literature I'd been teaching had comprised standard nineteenth century authors such as Pushkin, Gogol, Dostoevsky and Chekhov. Trying to appreciate socialist realist literature was quite challenging because of the background against which it was written. You have to be familiar with what was happening in Russia in the 1920s and 30s to comprehend the significance of the writers of the time and the difficulties they faced: speak out of turn and you could end up in a labour camp or even be shot. The other requirement of the course was to submit a 20,000-word thesis. I chose to present a comparative study of the treatment of mentally handicapped children in England and the Soviet Union. Hardly a laugh-a-minute topic.

Going back to university ten years after taking my first degree was an exhilarating experience. The undergrads accepted me as one of them despite the age difference and I enjoyed campus life. But I could see in them 'myself when young' and made no attempt to pretend that I was that age again and take part in silly student pranks – done all that, got the photos to prove it. I didn't make passes at girls a decade younger than myself just because we were chatting in the Common Room or perhaps sharing a table for lunch. I was a married man in his thirties with two children and in the process of adopting a third. Even the supervisor guiding our studies was younger than me.

This was at the time of the war in Vietnam and a lot of students were mightily upset by American involvement and the rumours of atrocities. In common with other student campuses, they wanted to express their hostility. The extreme elements got their chance when a speaker from the US embassy was invited to address a meeting, which he attended in the company of his daughter. The anti-American cohort lay in wait, ambushed the couple and doused them with red paint.

Most students were appalled and there was a lot of highly charged debate as to what to do. Were the speaker and his daughter fair game, representatives of an imperialist regime, so they got what they deserved? It could have been a lot worse – at least they weren't struck by missiles or threatened with weapons. On the other hand, they were at the university by invitation, so didn't that amount to a safe conduct, a flag of truce meaning no harm would come to an invited guest?

The atmosphere was super-charged, with feelings on both sides running high and a widespread feeling of apprehension that things could go badly wrong. If no steps were taken to distance the rest of the student body from the small group of extremists responsible for throwing the paint, then that meant that the Student Union tacitly accepted violence on campus and curbs on the free expression of opinion.

What next?

I heard about all of this in the departmental Common Room and that it had been suggested that an Extraordinary General Meeting of the Student Union be called and a motion put to condemn the assault on the spokesman and his daughter.

However, those who'd been responsible for the symbolic attack made it quite clear that if anyone made a move to put this idea into practice by putting their name to a motion as willing to propose or second it, this would be deemed to be showing support for American imperialism. Retribution would follow. As a result, everyone was running scared and no one would risk proposing any motion.

"Put my name as proposing it," I said. "To start with, no one will know who I am or where to find me. On top of that, I'm not some teenager fresh out of school but a mature adult with a family and a job. I've also spent time in the Royal Navy during national service, and am not likely to be intimidated by a handful of puffed-up, self-regarding students."

I found a seconder. He agreed to do so provided he didn't have to speak, fearing, I presume, some act of aggression.

Nonetheless, intimidation was attempted. The lefties invited me to meet them and suggested various ways to re-word the motion to make it acceptable to them by inserting some element criticising American involvement in Vietnam and side-stepping the principle of free speech. I stood my ground and refused point-blank to play their little game. But reasoned argument was futile. I disagreed with them, they squealed, because "you don't understand!" From their standpoint, if I agreed with them that proved that I understood, and if I didn't agree then that proved that I didn't – a circular argument in which reason and logic played no part. When they found that I was determined to stick with my wording they warned me that they would oppose the motion with might and main. "You do that," I said, "and we'll see who carries the day."

I knew from past experience that the amount of hot air produced by loud-mouths is usually in inverse proportion to the number of people spouting it. They and their threats, to quote a well-known cliché, are likely to be 'all piss and wind'. Large posters appeared on common room walls announcing the next meeting of 'the 8th February Committee' or 'the 15th February Committee'. Portentous as these may have appeared, in practice these 'committees' comprised a self-selected handful of misfit ideologues who rotated the roles of chairman, secretary and treasurer amongst themselves. They were 'Potemkin villages', so to speak. There may have been a committee, but it represented no one but those sitting around the table and there had been no elections to office because there weren't any other members to cast a vote.

Then the rightists invited me to meet them and offered me protection. I told them thanks, but no thanks. "I don't need protection. I live off campus well away from Brighton where they'll never find me and at weekends I'm back home in Hampshire."

Came the day, the chamber was so packed that I had difficulty getting in. A chap on the door tried to stop me. "It's full. You can't go in," he told me. "Well, I think I can," I responded rather tartly. "I'm proposing the motion." With his mouth sagging with disbelief, he stood aside. But he was right about it being a full house. Every seat was taken and those without seats were sitting on every available floor space. I had the devil's own job picking my way through the bodies, trying to avoid falling over on top of someone.

The meeting began with a procedural motion 'that the motion be not put', the grounds being that it didn't mention Vietnam, the War, the unjustified American invasion or the paint-throwing incident. They were right. I had deliberately worded the motion to be all-embracing, expressing a universal right to free speech, not forfeit if a bunch of students got all worked up about one particular topic.

The attempt to prevent the debate taking place was rejected by a large majority and I was permitted at last to take the floor and propose the motion that "This Union expresses its wholehearted and unequivocal support for the principles of free speech and free expression of opinion, coupled with equally wholehearted and unequivocal condemnation of any physical attack or assault of whatever kind upon any person or persons following their implementation of either of these freedoms."

The lefties were beside themselves with self-righteous spleen. How dare anyone propose such a motion when everyone knew that the American imperialists were committing atrocities in Vietnam and if their flunkey and his daughter dared to show their faces on the campus, they had it coming to them, etc., etc.

I stuck to my guns, defending the general principle of freedom of expression and refusing to be drawn into debating American aggression, the justification of retribution (throwing paint) or any of the other causes beloved of the lefties. They couldn't see the anomaly of demanding free speech for themselves to speak out against things they objected to while demanding that those who saw things differently be denied a hearing.

My assumption proved correct that the lefties were a vociferous but tiny minority and that their threats to overwhelm me if I dared to put such a general motion were hot air. For all their bluster, they could muster only 25 votes against the motion. Those in favour numbered in excess of 1200.

Experience has taught me that when shouty people claim to be speaking for the majority such a claim is at the very least tendentious and it's more than likely that the opposite is the case. The only people they've consulted are those who agree with them and they consciously ignore those who take a different view.

Calling their bluff on this occasion and on as public a platform as one could imagine stood me in good stead in my subsequent career as a local councillor and in due course chairman of the Planning Committee. On occasions too numerous to mention I found myself and my fellow committee members, alongside council staff, confronted by a shrieking mob of residents demanding that some planning application or other be thrown out because they were against it. If the committee, having listened to all the objections and heard the advice of the professionals decided to grant the application in spite of the objections, often all hell would break out and we'd be accused of – their favourite and hackneyed phrase – 'not listening to the people'. In truth the opposite was the case. I and the other committee members had 'listened to the people' at great length. What they couldn't understand was that the answer was 'no'.

Perhaps you've experienced similar situations in your work when you've had to make an unpopular decision, even though you knew that it was the right one.

But probably you haven't had to stand up in front of a student audience of some 1250 and single-handedly face down a raucous caucus utterly convinced of their own righteousness, all attempting to shout down anyone with an opposing view.

Consider yourself fortunate indeed!

29 February 1968

NB The Epilogue is another twist in this particular tale.

Postscript

St Mary's Church had so few worshippers attending services that it was declared redundant and in due course demolished. However, it had a splendid nineteenth century organ, which was rescued and given to the local hospital and installed in their chapel.

It was the largest organ donation that the hospital had ever received.

Goodnight.

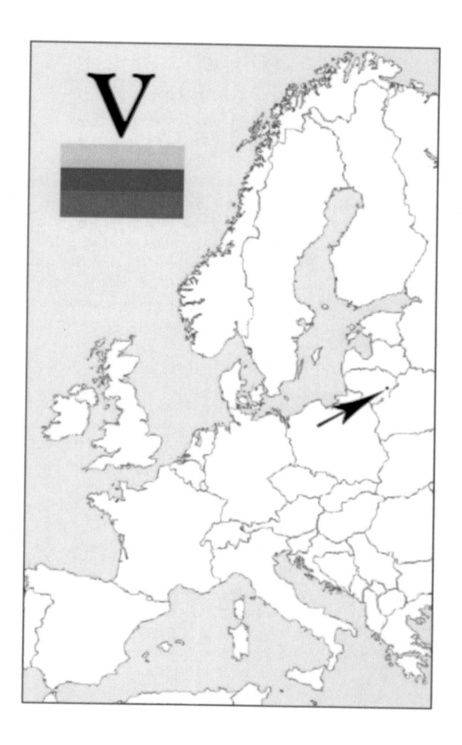

Vilnius

Seeing the Back of the King

[Conversations in italics were in Russian]

We arrived on the bus from Siauliai*. It stopped at the barrier at the bus terminal and waited for the attendant to raise the bar. We alighted at what looked like the back of a row of shops. We couldn't see any signs showing the way out or where the taxi rank was. The first door we tried led into a shopping mall and the information desk there was solely for the assistance of shoppers and had nothing to do with the buses or taxis. We retraced our steps and opted to have coffee in a small café which had enough space for our luggage while we planned our next move. It was a counter where you queued and paid the cashier when your tray had passed muster.

"How are we going to get to our hotel?" asked Mike. "There has to be a taxi rank *somewhere*."

"Stay here," I said. "Finish your coffee and guard the bags. I'll go and do a 'recce'. If there are no taxis waiting out front, I guess they must use this back area where our bus dropped us."

I saw a few, but the trouble was, any taxis dropping passengers immediately drove off again instead of waiting for possible new fares. I climbed some steps up an embankment onto a main road, hoping that perhaps that was where the taxis lined up. But no, nothing doing. Back down again.

As I reached the bottom of the stairs I noticed a taxi pausing at the entrance barrier to the bus terminal to speak to the girl in the kiosk.

"Ah!" I thought. "Incoming taxis have to stop at the barrier. If I go and wait there and catch one while he's stopped maybe I can get him to take us as his next fare."

When the next taxi stopped, I at once ran up to the driver's window.

"Are you free?" I asked, first in English, then in Russian, on the basis that if he didn't understand the first language, he'd certainly understand the second. When Lithuania was part of the Soviet Union, Russian was widely used as the language of the government and administration, as well as in higher education and in the Army where young men were conscripted.

"Da," he replied. Clearly, he preferred Russian.

"I want the Hotel Europa Royale. My luggage is in the café with my friend. Will you wait while I fetch him?"

He nodded.

We drove up to the waiting area to the rear of the shops.

"OK? I'll go and find my friend and collect our bags."

I dashed off to the café.

"I've got us a taxi," I gasped to Mike. "Quick!"

I grabbed my bags and we both hurried out. Our taxi was waiting dutifully. I sat beside the driver, who started to tell us, in a thick accent, about his past career as a lorry driver which had taken him all over the continent, including the UK. We'd assumed that a taxi driver in the capital of Lithuania would be a Lithuanian, but no – this fellow was a Chechen from the Caucasus. Getting out his iPad, he proceeded to show us pictures of himself in London and back home in Grozny, all the time continuing to drive. When he dropped us at the hotel, I felt quite relieved and that we'd arrived in one piece.

Our first experience of daily life in Vilnius was a mildly unpleasant revelation. After dinner we'd gone to sit at one of the hotel's outside tables to have coffee so that I could have a smoke. Much to our dismay, we were accosted by a beggar and then ten minutes later by another one. Worse was to come. Two young men were walking briskly up on the other side of the road when one of them peeled off, came over and stood in front of us, held out his hand for money and addressed us in what I presume was Lithuanian.

We told him firmly 'no'. What struck us both was that he wasn't some old man down on his luck perhaps with no pension struggling to keep body and soul together but a strapping young chap with no doubt a day job who, seeing a couple of tourists sitting outside a hotel enjoying a coffee, thought it perfectly acceptable behaviour to walk over, stick out his hand and try to cadge some money off them.

As befits a capital city, the historic parts of Vilnius extend over a considerable area but our agents had assured us that we'd be accommodated in the heart of the Old Town. The following morning our guide arrived at the hotel. She introduced herself as Regina* and at the same time informed us that she also guided in Spanish. She led the way on a walking tour, explaining that the city had always been cosmopolitan and hence there were Catholic, Orthodox, Uniate and Lutheran cathedrals all close to each other. In former times there had also been a mosque and in the days when 30% of the city's population were Jews, two synagogues.

The 'Gates of Dawn' are the last surviving of the five gates to the city in medieval times.

"Vilnius's Jews were among those worst affected by Hitler's 'final solution'," Regina told us. "They were virtually wiped out as the Gestapo went door to door systematically killing the occupants or rounding families up to be deported to concentration camps."

The city itself, however, was largely spared the physical destruction which utterly destroyed Klaipeda* and to a lesser extent Kaunas*, Lithuania's other main centres of population, during the struggle for independence from Tsarist Russia and then the war with Poland in the early 1920s. The medieval street pattern and the major eighteenth and nineteenth century buildings largely survive, even if converted to offices, hotels, shops or cafés.

The following day Regina drove us to the famous castle of Trakai*, once an important fortification and in times of trouble, a royal residence.

"It looks like a fairy-tale castle, Mike," I said, when I caught sight of it for the first time. "It's in the middle of a lake, not merely surrounded by a moat. You can see why the site was chosen."

"We have to cross that long bridge," he said, pointing across the lake. "It must have been virtually impregnable in its day. I'll take some shots from the shore here, and then about halfway across I can get the towers from different angles."

We'd only got about halfway across when our attention was diverted by a dozen ducks on the lake engaged in a pitched battle! There was no obvious cause, but much flapping of wings, angry quacking and crash landings.

"Looks like the avian version of World War Three has arrived," observed Mike.

We reached the entrance to the castle, which lay through an archway flanked by curtain walls and massive towers.

"The upper parts are all restorations," Regina was at pains to point out. "They're trying to re-create it as it would have been in its heyday the fourteenth century. The colour of the bricks has been retained, but you can see the line between the surviving original bricks and the reconstruction. There's no attempt to deceive."

Inside the castle was an open courtyard with a gallery and a flight of external wooden stairs giving access to the upper floor. Only two rooms in the castle were connected: The Grand Duke's private quarters and those of the Grand Duchess. This strengthened the castle's defences because attackers would have to clear each room individually and then come out into the corridor or passageway exposing themselves to danger and proceed to the next one.

"In fact," said Regina, "the castle was never captured by force. When it ceased to have any military value, it was abandoned and the locals plundered it for stone and bricks to build their own houses."

The final day of our visit was to the former palace of the Grand Dukes, dating from medieval times when at the height of its powers Lithuania stretched from the Baltic almost to the Black Sea. The palace fell into decay following wars in the 17th and 18th centuries when Lithuania came under Russian control and Vilnius ceased to be the seat of government. In 1801 the Tsarist régime deliberately destroyed what was left – even selling the bricks!

"When Lithuania regained its independence, archaeologists were sent in to carry out a survey," said Regina. "They uncovered the original foundations, opened them up under glass and installed walkways so that visitors can see them."

She went on: "The palace has been rebuilt on top of these original foundations, and is part museum and part restored state rooms hung with tapestries."

I turned to Mike. "Have you seen these information panels? They're in Lithuanian and English and for a change, in spot-on correct English! The narrative starts from Lithuania's first appearance in records in the thirteenth century and tells the story of the country's history right up to the eighteenth century when it was swallowed up by Prussia and Russia in the Partitions of Poland."

The exhibits explained the struggles of the Grand Dukes in medieval times against their neighbours: the Teutonic Knights in the north and the Poles to the south. The contest with Poland was effectively concluded when the Grand Duke Jagiełło* became King of Poland in 1386 and Poland-Lithuania was at the time the largest state in Europe. He then crushed the Knights at the Battle of Grunwald* in 1410, a defeat from which they never recovered. This ushered in a 'golden age' for Poland-Lithuania which lasted nearly two hundred years.

We could see that restoration of the palace to its original proportions and opulence on its original site is well under way. Modern Lithuania is proud of its history.

"There are state rooms on the second floor," Regina told us.

"Can we see them?" I asked.

"Unfortunately, they're closed today as the King of Sweden is here on an official visit."

As we made our way slowly back to the hotel, we stopped at a café in the wide main road. While we were sitting outside wrapped in blankets against the chill, a motorcade with motorcycle outriders approached from the top of the hill. By sheer chance we were sitting directly opposite the Swedish embassy, recognisable from the national coat of arms above the entrance. From the second car with national flags on the bumpers who should alight to visit his embassy but King Carl Gustaf himself! We could just glimpse the back of his head as he entered the building, surrounded by staff and security.

"Mike," I said, "who'd have thought that we'd come to the capital of Lithuania and see of all people the King of Sweden!"

"It's an incredible coincidence," he replied. "You couldn't make it up."

October 2015

Pronunciation Guide

Grunwald:	**Groon**-*valt*
Jagiełło:	*Yag-**yeah**-whoa*
Kaunas:	**Cow**-*nass*
Klaipeda:	**Kly**-*ped-a (as in 'sky')*
Regina:	*Regg-**een**-a*
Siauliai:	**Shaw**-*lee-ay*
Trakai:	**Track**-*ay*
Vilnius:	**Veel**-*nee-oos*

[Adapted from 'Jottings from Russia and the Baltic States. Part 2: Latvia, Lithuania and Finland'. Other books are listed inside the front cover.]

Postscript

Lady of the house (to maid):	"Mary, there's so much dust on this piano I can write my name in it."
Mary:	"Yes, Ma'am. Education's a wonderful thing."

Goodnight.

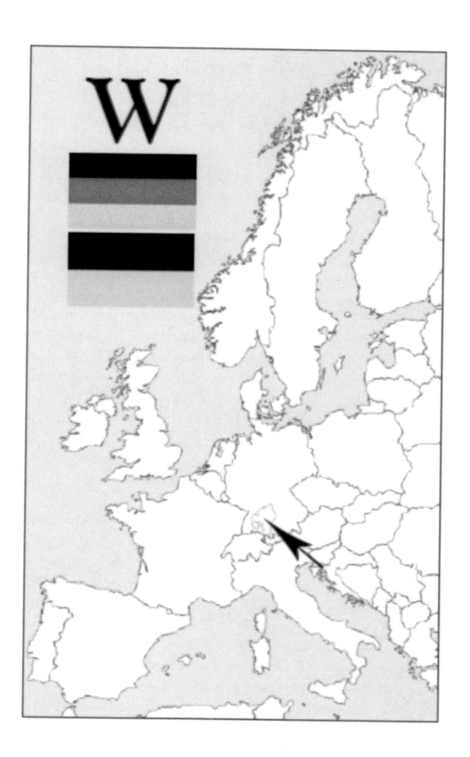

Württemberg

Twinning with a Vengeance
or Rather, Without

My connection with this part of south-western Germany extends over four decades. In 1963 my adopted home town of Eastleigh twinned with Villeneuve-St-Georges near Paris, and as Villeneuve was already twinned with Kornwestheim, a satellite town of Stuttgart, state capital of Baden-Württemberg, in 1978 we decided to twin with them, too. Their mayor – the *Oberbürgermeister* – was invited to bring a delegation to England to sign the appropriate documents.

Since then it has become our custom to invite each other to commemorate together the Armistice which brought to an end the First World War. Wreaths are laid and speeches delivered extolling the bravery and sacrifice of those who died, including nowadays those who suffered or died in the Second World War and in all other conflicts since.

In France the Armistice is celebrated on 11 November regardless of which day of the week it falls on, but in England we opt for the nearest Sunday and in Germany they mark the occasion on the Sunday after. Occasionally this leads to clashes of dates. When this happens our mayor leads the ceremonies here and we send the deputy mayor to represent us in our twin town.

In Eastleigh the mayor, wearing the robes and chain of office, leads a procession on a short walk from our former town hall to the war memorial on our town centre recreation ground. There, veterans' groups, uniformed youth organisations such as scouts, guides and army and air force cadets are lined up on parade on the other three sides of the memorial, ready to lay their wreaths after the official party have laid theirs. There is usually a large crowd of townsfolk present to pay their respects.

The mayoral procession is in strict order: the mace bearer, the mayor, accompanied by his wife (or husband, if the mayor is a woman), our civic guests from the twin towns, the mayor's chaplain, the council's chief executive, the local MP, freemen of the borough, citizens of honour and past mayors wearing their civic medals and finally current councillors. As a past mayor myself, I take my place in the line-up each year.

On arrival at the war memorial, the Last Post is sounded from our bandstand and a minute's silence observed. The mayor then delivers his speech, followed by the French and German delegates speaking in English if they can, otherwise in their own languages followed by a translation delivered on their behalf by a colleague.

During the remainder of the weekend, each mayor extends hospitality to our guests and takes the opportunity to show them something of their town or its neighbourhood. Forty years ago, Eastleigh was a major centre for railway construction and our visitors were likely to be shown around the railway works. In more recent times we have entertained them at a reception at the Ageas Bowl, home of Hampshire County Cricket Club which, despite being publicised when matches are being played as being 'at Southampton', is in fact located a mile outside the city's boundaries and entirely within the borough of Eastleigh. Alternatively, we may take them to Southampton to see the medieval walls or perhaps farther afield to Portsmouth Dockyard to visit HMS *Victory* or to Winchester to see the cathedral.

I still remember with a smile being taken by our German hosts to the beer festival near Stuttgart, Canstatterfest. Because my wife Margaret, mayor at the time, spoke reasonable German, Ernst Fischer, the Oberbürgermeister, felt sufficiently at ease with her to buy her a cardboard heart on a string from one of the stalls and hang it around her neck while the rest of us put on festive hats. Written on the heart in large letters were the words *'Dufte Biene'*. He neglected to tell her what this meant. When she found out that she'd been walking around the festival wearing a sign in dialect for which the nearest translation is 'I'm a smasher!' she put on a show of mock offence. 'What do you mean, *'Dufte Biene'*? I'll have you know I'm the Mayor of Eastleigh!' But in fact she took the joke in good part. It showed that Anglo-German relations were in a pretty healthy state when the host felt it was perfectly safe to play a practical joke on his visiting dignitary.

On another occasion, knowing of my interest in history, he took us across the state border to Rothenburg ob der Tauber in Bavaria where there is a famous astronomical clock with revolving figures similar to the perhaps better-known example in Prague. Unfortunately, it was pouring with rain and we hadn't really an adequate supply of large umbrellas so were rather preoccupied with trying to keep dry when we should have been giving the ingenious clock our full attention as it struck the hour and the figures processed.

The significance of Rothenburg today lies in the fact that it has survived from the Middle Ages more or less intact. Most of the towns in this part of Germany were sacked and burnt during the Thirty Years' War between Protestants and Catholics which raged from 1618–48, some of them more than once, as armies advanced or retreated. The story goes that when a Catholic army lay siege to Protestant Rothenburg the bürgermeister was challenged to empty a three-quarters of a litre flagon of wine with the promise that if he did so the besiegers would refrain from sacking the town. It is to his success in meeting this challenge that Rothenburg owes its remarkable state of preservation. The truth is more prosaic: the town had to pay a huge bribe. But whichever it was, the town was spared and stands today as a rare medieval survival.

On another visit Herr Fischer took us to Esslingen, some 20km distant, for lunch in a restaurant truly evocative of rural Swabia and on another occasion to the restaurant halfway up the local TV tower. On another visit to Kornwestheim we were delayed by bad weather, landed at Frankfurt airport instead of Stuttgart and had a long drive by minibus and finally arrived in Kornwestheim at about ten o'clock in the evening having been up since five in the morning. At the hotel we took our luggage up to our rooms and came down to find a banquet laid out. To this day I cannot fathom how, along with all the dishes of vegetables one would expect, preceded by wine and entrées and finally seemingly boundless choices of dessert, there could have been fifteen different sorts of meat on offer. Needless to say, we were all exhausted and in no fit state to do justice to such a spread, but good manners decreed that we make an effort for the sake of appearances. Our hosts had intended to give us a warm welcome and had laid on a fine dinner. It wasn't their fault that we arrived five hours later than planned.

Kornwestheim has an unusual Rathaus, or town hall, built as a square tower between 1933–5 and where only the first four storeys are actually used. Opposite is the main public hall, where on every visit I can remember we have been entertained by the town's brass band or we've sat at long tables quaffing beer or wine while musicians played traditional country music of the 'oompah band' variety. We all had a great time and some of us even accepted invitations to join in the local dances!

The author with M. Raymond Vincelot, Maire-deputé of Villeneuve-St-Georges with responsibility for twinning. In the background, the Rathaus at Kornwestheim, 1933–5.

For many years we in Eastleigh boasted a popular concert troupe, the Southern Minstrels, who would perform in Eastleigh, sharing the programme with the Sangerlust choir from Kornwestheim. The following year, the Minstrels would go to Kornwestheim and join the performance on stage there. Sadly, this came to an end when Iris Price, who ran the Minstrels, finally decided that it was time to retire and without her the ensemble folded.

We also used to send troupes of our baton twirling girls. Kornwestheim once sent us some teenage girls dressed in a stage adaptation of the uniform worn by the Duke's personal guard in the eighteenth century, with hip-length fur-trimmed coats, tricorn hats with feathers and fishnet stockings in lieu of breeches and hose. They called themselves the Red Guard, the Green Guard or the Blue Guard according to the colour of their costumes. They performed some extremely well-rehearsed dance routines and were rewarded with a standing ovation.

The author with Iris Price whose Southern Minstrels exchanged visits and performed alongside the Sangerlust (a choir based in Kornwestheim).

I've happily lived in Chandler's Ford in the borough of Eastleigh for over fifty years and would never pretend that we have much of interest to show to an ordinary tourist. The ruins of Netley Abbey indicate a substantial monastic establishment in the Middle Ages, but prior to the mid-to-late nineteenth century most of the borough was farmland or woodland. We have a working windmill in Bursledon dating from the early nineteenth century, which is managed by a joint committee of borough and county councillors and of which I once served as chairman. Botley Square is dominated by the classical columns of the Grade II Listed Market Hall, but it dates only from 1848.

Much the same can be said of Kornwestheim. The half-timbered houses in its old quarter are evidence of an earlier flourishing rural community. Only when industry arrived at the end of the nineteenth century with the Salamander shoe-making factory did population growth turn it into a town.

Lack of tourist attractions does not detract from the value of town twinning if undertaken with serious intent. Towns and cities with historic buildings to show off have no difficulty in marketing themselves or twinning with equally spectacular towns and cities in other countries. However, the purpose of twinning with a foreign town is not simply to show off your own town's wonders in between booze-ups. It's to learn about the way of life in the other society and in so doing foster mutual understanding and respect. It's to encourage the people of each town to visit the other and get to know it and the people who live there, whether going as a tourist, a member of a choir, a dance or theatre group, a church, a musician, a sportsman or woman or, as I have on several occasions, officially as a civic representative. Cynics knowing nothing about the reality of twinning customarily sniff and dismiss exchange visits as just 'a jolly'.

Pillar showing Kornwest-heim's four twin towns.

Perhaps for some that's all it is, particularly first-time visitors who'll never visit again, but for other participants the purpose is more serious. Enjoy yourself, of course, and if you're the host, then entertain your guests hospitably as best you can. If you're the guest then show appreciation of whatever church, museum, factory or children's art exhibition your hosts show you and learn something about the foreign culture into which you have been temporarily immersed. Beyond being entertained by your hosts, learning about their lifestyle and customs requires focused application. We all know people who visit many countries but return none the wiser, bringing nothing back from their travels except 'selfies' and a suntan.

In the formal celebration in Kornwestheim of forty years of twinning in 2018, gifts were exchanged and honorific speeches delivered – including my own as secretary of the Twinning Association. We were taken to Stuttgart to see the city's refurbished museum and an exhibition by a local sculptor and artist, then lunch and in the evening enjoyed the customary brass band concert.

On Sunday there was a service of commemoration in the Lutheran church, during which the minister conducted a christening. We then drove in a convoy to the cemetery to be greeted by a wind band and choir. This was followed by speeches from the Oberbürgermeisterin and representatives from three of Kornwestheims's four twin towns (the Russians from Kimry were not in attendance). Then giant civic wreaths each held by two uniformed bearers marching in step were carried in procession to a slow drumbeat. After the ceremony was over we went to lunch in a different restaurant from the night before, where we met representatives of the local US Army base. In the afternoon I enjoyed an optional walking tour of the old quarter, following which the official parties – English and French – departed to catch planes or trains home.

I stayed on for a brief private visit, to stroll on my own around the town and do a bit of shopping. This gave me the opportunity to pick up some good ideas which I wouldn't have known about had I not been taking part in a twinning visit. For this reason, I took photographs of public seating and imaginative children's play equipment to bring to the attention of my parish council colleagues back home. I figured that if Kornwestheim could provide comfort for its ordinary citizens and amusement for its children while meeting health and safety regulations then there was no reason to doubt that we could do the same in Chandler's Ford.

I rest my case.

April 1978, November 2018 and several times in between!

Postscript

Q: Why it is that chicks don't cost very much to buy in the market?

A: Because they're always going *'cheep'*.

Q: Why is it that when they get older and become chickens, they're still don't cost very much?

A: Because you can always buy chickens for a poultry sum.

Goodnight.

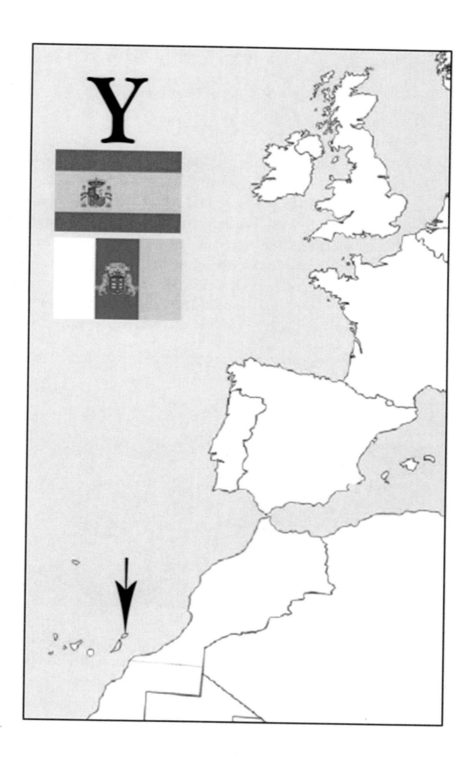

YE

Be Sure Ye Are Covered

For twenty-five years I had a time-share in the Canaries, in Lanzarote. In the north of the island is marked on the map a name which has always amused me: a place called simply 'Yé'. It must be in line for a place in the record books for being the settlement with the world's shortest name.

More of a mystery, when driving along the road and seeing the sign indicating that you are now entering Yé, you drive past about four houses, spread either side of the road, and quickly reach another sign facing the other way. You are now leaving Yé. Blink, and you'd miss it. There are no public buildings, no village centre, in reality no village. Just a name on a pole beside the road.

What I'd hoped to find most of all was an Anglican church, imagining the vicar on Christmas morning summoning his parishioners through a loud-hailer: "Our morning carol service is about to begin. O come, all Ye faithful."

Perhaps I'm word-playing this to death. Sorry. But I'm sure ye understand.

A more serious memory of Lanzarote dates from the previous year, when my daughter-in-law, Karen, and my friend Mike (of 'Siberia' fame) accompanied me. There was a bus to Órzola in the far north of the island, but it turned around straightaway for the return journey to Arrecife, the island capital, and that was it – no other bus later in the day to get you back. So, Mike hired a car and we drove up. There were several rather enticing restaurants near the ferry to the nearby island of La Graciosa where I fancied the fish menu.

During the days Mike drove, I sat beside him more or less motionless. I noted an intermittent numbness in my right arm. Cramp, I supposed. It began on Tuesday and continued from time to time on Wednesday. Mike and Karen flew home on Thursday, changeover day for tourists on Lanzarote, leaving me alone for the remaining week of my intended stay. I experienced the numbness again later in the day and thought to myself, "If this goes on tomorrow, I'm going to seek medical advice."

Friday dawned bright and clear and my arm was again intermittently numb. I went to Reception at my resort.

"Have you a first-aider on site?"

"Yes, sir. I'll ring for her."

Debi, responsible for residents' welfare, duly arrived. I explained my symptoms.

"You don't want the clinic in town," she said. "That's for people who've trodden on a piece of glass on the beach, or fallen downstairs because they'd over-indulged in sangria. You want a proper hospital. There's one only about ten minutes away. Pack a bag with your overnight things and I'll drive you there."

We arrived. Reception called one of the doctors on duty and we were ushered into a waiting area.

"We'll give you a scan," said the doctor, in heavily accented English.

After this procedure, I waited while the results were examined.

The doctor came over to me, sitting with Debi. "We're going to admit you to intensive care."

"You're WHAT?"

"You've had a mini-stroke. We need to assess what damage there may have been to your brain and monitor your blood pressure."

"I'll come and see you tomorrow," said Debi. "Do you want me to bring you anything?"

"Something to read, please."

"Assuming that I'm still here tomorrow," I was thinking. "'Mini-stroke'? Sounds ominous."

Admitted at a rate of knots, I was unceremoniously installed in the end bed on a ward and wired up to various contraptions which went 'Whoo! Whoo!' or 'Click, Click' or flashed lights of various colours. I had no idea what any of these machines were telling the medical staff. They brought me meals at suitable intervals and came every hour to take my blood pressure.

What a good job I'd brought some magazines to read. I felt perfectly OK, but underneath the surface calm the term 'mini-stroke' had got me worried. We've all heard of people who have had such experiences and suffer partial paralysis or their speech is slurred or they never recover full use of one side of their body afterwards. In my case, such an outcome would hardly be out of the ordinary, at the age of 79.

Hospitals are notorious for being places where patients can seldom enjoy a night's uninterrupted sleep. I cheerfully submitted to being woken hourly to have my blood pressure taken, as this was part of my treatment. But I got more and more frustrated and angry because at the far end of the ward an elderly woman kept crying out, 'Why are you keeping me here?' and then five minutes later, 'Why are you being so cruel to me?' and similar anguished cries for help all through the night. Apparently, she'd fallen ill aboard a cruise ship and been brought ashore for treatment, but was clearly not of sound mind and hence didn't understand that she was in a hospital. She kept the rest of the ward awake most of the night. This annoyed us all because we saw no reason why she couldn't have been given a sedative instead of one of the orderlies coming to her bedside at frequent intervals and saying to her in broken English, 'Go to sleep, madam,' as if that was going to make any difference to someone who was disoriented and frightened.

Debi kindly turned up with some reading matter and some fruit and three days later they transferred me to a recovery ward. I shared it with a Dutch gentleman and we struck up a conversation about my travels in Holland and his travels worldwide with his wife. She came to visit and expressed an interest in having one of my books. I offered to post one on my return to England and in due course received payment in euros. From my standpoint as an author, my time in hospital wasn't entirely wasted.

On discharge, they gave me a prescription list to take to a pharmacy. When I got back to my apartment and unpacked my bag of boxes, I discovered to my surprise that it included eight syringe doses which I was instructed to inject into my stomach. They hadn't warned me about that! Diabetics won't sympathise, but to the rest of us pinching one's flesh into a lump and sticking a needle in it oneself is a bit daunting the first time. But I steeled myself. After all, it was only eight doses and was for my own good. Best grit the teeth, squeeze the paunch and get it over with.

My insurers insisted that my discharge be contingent on having someone else staying with me in the flat and the upshot was that I had to ring Karen in England and ask her if she could come back for a week just to be a presence. She arrived and the hospital discharged me. We then had to wait a week to get a flight. I phoned a friend at home who was a patient at the same surgery and asked him to arrange for me to see my own doctor the day after I arrived back in England.

The insurers, belt and braces, sent out a doctor to travel back with me, conduct me to the airport and arrange for me to be taken on board the aircraft in a wheelchair, with an oxygen tube attached to my nose and a small cylinder placed on the empty seat beside me. He had an interesting background. He came originally from South Sudan, and had several brothers, similarly highly qualified, scattered around the world. He revealed that accompanying me was of professional interest because he was carrying out research into blood pressure and trying to discover whether or not it was possible to have different pressure in different parts of the body at the same time. On arrival at Gatwick a wheelchair was once again provided. As his contract stated that he had to accompany me all the way home, a taxi was waiting. You may not be surprised to learn that once again I grasped an opportunity: I sold him a book. Next morning, I took up my appointment with my own doctor and showed him the hospital notes. They were in Spanish but the medical terms were much the same. He immediately arranged for me to see a specialist at the county hospital. Within ten days I had a consultation and three weeks later an operation to clear out my right carotid artery.

The after effects were quite dramatic. My eyes didn't focus properly and I found it impossible to read. My doctor advised me not to drive for a month and to cancel my road fund licence.

Three weeks later I saw the specialist again, to see if the operation had been a success. It had.

"I shall have to do the other one in about five years' time," he told me. His voice dropped, as he adopted a confidential tone. "You will be here in five years' time, won't you?"

"Well, I wasn't planning the alternative."

He laughed out loud.

"I'd rather you did it now, while I'm comparatively fit and healthy. I may not be so fit in five years' time at 85."

He thought for a moment. "I'll fit you in in September."

"Sorry. I'll be in Mongolia."

He stopped dead in his tracks. "Where?"

"I'm planning a trip on the Trans-Siberian Railway and we plan a diversion across Mongolia and we'll then fly home from Beijing. It's all booked."

"When you get back, then."

In due course my operation to clear out the other carotid was scheduled for October. It was then cancelled due to beds not being available because of emergencies and was finally carried out a fortnight late.

I cancelled my car licence for a month, expecting to suffer the same after-effects as followed the first operation, only more so.

Five days later I saw the specialist for a post-operative check-up.

"You're fine. Your chances of a heart attack now go down from 20% to two. You're fit to drive if you want to."

This was, of course, excellent news, but bitter-sweet as I now had to persuade the DVLA, the licensing authority, to cancel my cancellation, as it were, and re-issue my road fund licence. It was quite a rigmarole, but pointed up a remarkable disparity between the effects of the first operation and the effects of the second. One would expect to suffer more after the second than the first but the opposite occurred. To all intents and purposes, I suffered no ill-effects after the second operation. My eyes weren't affected, my appetite remained normal and I was, as the cliché has it, 'right as rain'.

'Be thankful for small mercies', I can imagine you muttering to yourself. And you'd be right.

The lesson from this tale is this: when travelling abroad, be sure to have good health insurance. I was told afterwards that my hospital expenses were £1,000 per night. Those costs, the doctor beside me on my flight home and the taxi from Gatwick to my front door, were all covered.

February 2013

Postscript

Henry Brownlow was a professional make-up artist. He was rather jealous of his beautiful wife, Rachel, and became suspicious when she began to visit the local hospital to see the consultant gynaecologist, Mr Hamworth, who cut a dashing figure with his dapper attire and trim moustache.

When Rachel was called to the hospital yet again, Henry's suspicions became unbearable and he decided to act on them. He made himself up to look like his wife, donned a wig and one of her dresses and turned up for the appointment in her place, unaware that it was not a consultation but for surgery.

Henry came round in the recovery ward and the following conversation took place.

"Where am I?" he asked the nurse.

"You're in the recovery ward, Mr Brownlow," she replied.

At that point, Mr Hamworth came into the ward, doing his rounds.

"Ah, Mr Brownlow," he said. "You're a make-up artist, aren't you? You're really, really good. You had us completely fooled right up to the last minute, and by then it was too late to stop the procedure. So now you're going to be in the Guinness Book of Records."

"Why's that?" asked Henry.

"You're the first man in the world to have a hysterectomy."

I bid Ye 'Goodnight'.

Zagreb

Lost on A Train in Western Bosnia

Bob and I had volunteered for a stint working in a refugee camp in Austria, but planned to get visas for Yugoslavia for a week's visit before our start date at the camp near Linz. Not work, then free time for a holiday, but the other way round. We took the train from Salzburg to Graz to pick up the overnight express from Vienna to Istanbul via Zagreb where we changed trains. These were very exotic names in the 1950s, though ten a penny now with independent Croatia a popular tourist destination.

What struck us most on arrival was that we didn't appear to have left Austria – the architecture was exactly the same in Zagreb as it was in Graz or Salzburg. On reflection, it isn't hard to understand why. The whole of this part of Europe was for centuries part of the Habsburg Empire and all three towns were in the same country – sort of.

The main reason for staying overnight in Zagreb was to see Croatia's principal church, the Cathedral of the Assumption of the Virgin Mary. It was originally constructed in the thirteenth century but the present building is modern, built in Gothic style following a disastrous earthquake in 1880. On a wall inside is a huge inscription written in Glagolitic script, the earliest attempt by Christian missionaries, probably in the ninth century, to represent the sounds in Slavonic languages. Modern scholars believe that it pre-dates the Cyrillic script used nowadays for writing Russian and, with modifications, for writing in Belarusian, Ukrainian and Bulgarian (and also for writing modern Mongolian, even though it is not a Slavonic language!). Serbs, Croats and Bosnians speak virtually the same language – Serbo-Croat – but the Serbs write it using yet another modification of Cyrillic while in Croatia and Bosnia-Herzegovina the Latin alphabet is used.

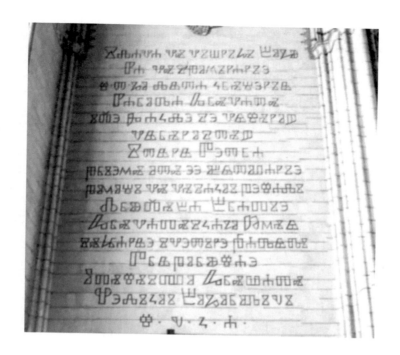

Next day we caught the train to Sarajevo, and in due course found that we had made one fatal mistake. We were on the right train, yes. What we hadn't realised was that at some point it separated into two sections and we'd seated ourselves in the wrong end. I'll leave you in suspense for the time being as to how this was going to turn out.

Our journey did not begin without incident. We were seated next to three generations of a family: grandmother, mother and baby, who occupied the window seats. Bob was next to the grandmother; I was alongside the mother with the baby on her lap. That she was what we would call a nursing mother became apparent when after half an hour the baby cried and she immediately whopped out the starboard breast and popped her nipple into the baby's mouth. 'Women's lib' has ensured that nowadays meeting the natural needs of a child in such a direct way is more or less acceptable with a bit of discretion, but back in the 50s it was quite a culture shock and not the sort of thing one saw every day on the Bakerloo Line. I was aware that we were well and truly 'in foreign', where things were different.

Suddenly Bob lurched towards me away from the grandmother, his face contorted as though in his death agonies.

"What's up?"

"She's just dropped her guts!"

What got him, apart from the smell, was that the elderly lady responsible had engulfed him in a noxious odour without making any sound and while staring out of the train window without even a hint of change in facial expression. Nor, of course, any word of apology. An industrial-strength smelly fart was all part of a normal day on a Bosnian train and nothing to pass comment about. 'In foreign', again.

The family got off shortly after, taking baby and fart with them, I moved over to sit alongside Bob and a couple in their late thirties took the seats opposite. After an exchange of smiles – Westerners weren't all that common on Yugoslav trains and we were a bit of a novelty – the man produced a bottle of slivovic, the local plum brandy, took a swig and passed it to his wife. She took a swig, passed it back, he took another swig and then leaned across and passed it to me. 'In foreign', again. Hospitality to strangers in a way that the buttoned-up English would never dream of displaying. It would have been insulting to refuse. I took a gulp of the sweet, fermented liquid, whereupon it was indicated with a sweep of the hand that I should pass it not back but sideways to Bob. This went on until we'd gone through half the bottle.

We might have had no language in common, but this gesture indicated feelings of friendship and went a long way towards soothing Bob, who was still recovering from his brush with death by asphyxiation a few stations back.

When the couple got off, they were replaced by a couple of schoolgirls who hearing us talking in English began at once to try out theirs, which obviously they were learning at school. I exchanged addresses with one of them, and so acquired my first Balkan pen-friend, who according to the address she gave me was at school in Slavonski Brod. We swapped chatty letters for several years, but lost contact eventually as is the norm with pen friendships – though I began one in 1948 which lasted nearly forty years until, at the age of 87, my friend died. The difference there, though, is that he lived not in some far distant country but in Amsterdam and we exchanged not just letters but personal visits regularly. We got to know each other and each other's families so well that we became 'family' too.

I've never forgotten the Yugoslav girl's name, because she wrote it for me back to front as 'Dizdarevič Zebra'. The couple of moments it took me to realise that she had written her surname first and then Christian name had the effect of implanting it in my memory so firmly that more than half-a-century later the name and address of someone I met once and exchanged a few letters with over a few years is still fresh.

I occasionally wonder what happened to her. Did she carry on with her studies of English? Did she marry and have a family? How did the break-up of Yugoslavia affect her? Is she, even, still alive and living in the new independent Croatia? If so, call me!

Returning to our situation of being blissfully ignorant of the fact that we were in the wrong part of the train, at Banja Luka* it split without us being aware of what was happening as the announcements were in Serbo-Croat so we didn't understand them. The front half went on to Sarajevo, the back half, with us in it, went off up a branch line to Doboj*. Where? No, we'd never heard of it either, until we ended up on its station platform in semi-darkness clutching the wrong tickets. We'd realised that Plan A wasn't working when the names on the stations we passed through didn't match our map. Then as we approached Zenica*, the town immediately before Doboj, we were treated to a spectacular firework display from the chimneys of the local heavy engineering works.

"This isn't on the route to Sarajevo," we both thought. "So, what the hell are we doing here?" I said to Bob.

We were starring, obviously but unwittingly, in the block-busting B-list thriller 'Lost on a Train in Western Bosnia!' a sort of version of Hansel and Gretel but with rolling stock. Of course, as a result of the wars and ethnic cleansing campaigns in the 1990s everyone nowadays knows exactly where Bosnia is. When we made our trip in 1956 most people were pretty hazy about where Yugoslavia was, let alone Bosnia. Somewhere on the other side of the Iron Curtain, isn't it? Er, yes, sort of.

At Doboj we got off and Bob went in to try to find the stationmaster and enquire about trains to Sarajevo. Not speaking any Serbo-Croat (what foreigner does?) he used German – in fact, the only foreign language he knew. The effect was electric. The stationmaster sprang to attention, clicked his heels and shouted 'Ja wohl!' It would appear that five years of Nazi occupation had left their mark. He directed Bob to the correct platform, a train came and in due course we arrived safely in Sarajevo albeit several hours later than intended.

Then the fun really started, as you can read under S. In another book.

But this is Z.
Zzzzzzzzzzzz.

July 1956

Guide to Pronunciation

Banja Luka:	**Ban**-*yah* **Loo**-*ka*
Doboj:	*Dub*-**boy**
Zenica:	**Zen**-*ee-tsa*

I hope you've enjoyed the book. Thanks for reading it. I hope you'll enjoy the Epilogue.

Tomorrow.

Postscript

Two passengers were in a railway compartment when it passed a huge field of sheep.

First passenger: "Hey, look! I've never seen so many sheep in one field."

Second passenger: "Yes. There were 193 of them."

First passenger: "How could you possibly know that?"

Second passenger: "It was quite easy, really. I just counted their legs and divided by four."

Goodnight.

Epilogue

Following on from the extraordinary general meeting of the Sussex University Student Union (v. 'U') on 29 February 1968 the following article appeared in UNIONEWS, vol. X no 8 in March. When asked what I meant by an Icelandic carthorse I replied that it was 'cool, but clumsy'. The piece was a tongue-very-much-in-cheek, put-down of the self-righteous and humourless lefties, whose successors can still be found in today's society. The two bumbling old gaffers living in their own world and getting it wrong really got up their noses because they had no answer to ridicule other than to make threats of violence.

Parallel to the Vietnam War there were some domestic problems. The Vice-Chancellor, Prof. Asa Briggs, had made an unpopular decision (about student housing, I think) and as a result, some students took it upon themselves to stage a sit-in on the steps of the building where his office was located. His reaction to this intimidation really upset the demonstrators: he sent them out a tray of coffee and pastries! Other contemporary references in the article are to Ho Chi Minh, the leader of the Vietcong whom the Americans were fighting in Vietnam, LBJ who was Lyndon Baines Johnson, President of the United States at the time, and Prof. Christian Barnard who had recently carried out the first successful heart transplant.

The Icelandic Carthorse

(or 'La Carteblanche Elle 'n Dique')
A One-Act Triptych for Tinie-Whinies

Offered from a safe distance by MARTIN KYRLE (of whom it can be said), aided and aborted by STEVE KEY (spinster of this parish) and ELLEN WILLIAMS (who shall remain shameless).

THE SCENE is an Old Peoples' Home with fitted toilet and post office. Two Old Gaffers, Willmot and Harrison, are sitting in a doze in deckchairs, musing on the contemporary scene. In the distance can be dimly discerned a flight of steps leading to a sunken lawn. On the steps, a motley of gilded youth, abominable snowmen, fishmongers, warmongers, no-war mongers, standard bearers (some with high, others with low, standards), untouchables, unbearables, Old Uncle Tom Macobley, Jan Stewer and one other.

Applause

The two Old Gaffers wear baggy trousers, faded sports blazers with club badges and old straw hats with drooping brims which, like so many things, become limp with age and constant use. Harrison's knees are almost permanently crossed and reveal one shoelace dangling and that he is wearing odd socks. Both are rather hard of hearing, but neither likes to admit it and their speech is quavery and slurred. As the applause gets louder, Harrison partly wakes up.

Har. I say, Willmot, what's that noise? (*Renewed applause*).

Wil. Sorry, didn't I say pardon? I keep forgetting.

Har. No. There's applause. You're not applauding yourself, are you, Willmot?

Wil. I'll just wipe my spectacle.

(*He takes out a pair of spectacles with the left eyeglass missing and laboriously wipes the remaining one with a dirty handkerchief. He holds the spectacles up to his eyes, shuts his right eye and squints through the empty left socket). I can't see any noise. (More applause).*

Har. They're clapping again.

Wil. I think someone's done something. (*Renewed applause*). It must have been a good one.

Har. Can you see the scoreboard?

Wil. I don't know. There's a young feller down the front holding up a big card. Can't quite see it, though.

Har. (*With octogenarian enthusiasm, but to no one in particular*). Well played, sir!

Wil. That lawn didn't used to be big enough. They must have very short boundaries.

Har. Perhaps they have no limits at all.

Wil. I don't know.

Har. Perhaps they don't know the limits.

Wil. Should we tell them what the limits are?

(*He gets up with a great deal of effort, rubbing his back and scraping his chair on the concrete with a rasping noise. (Renewed applause. Distant chants of 'Asa Out', 'Asa Out') Willmot sits down, a gleam of understanding crawling slowly across his face.*

He's out! Harrison, he's out! I think they've stumped him.

Har. He must have jumped out too far that time. Doesn't do to overreach yourself.

(*Renewed chants of 'Asa Out!', 'Asa Out!'*)

Wil. I think he's appealing to the crowd.

Har. (*With disgust*). Bad sport that. In my young days no one ever appealed to the crowds. (*Renewed chants of 'Asa Out!', 'Asa Out!'*)

Wil. Ah! He's not appealing to *that* crowd.

Har. I don't suppose anyone would.

Wil. No.

Har. Who's in now?

(*Stands up and peers into the distance*). They're holding up another card. *Spells out slowly: V-I-E-T-N-A-M-E*). Feller by the name of Viet. Foreigner, by the sound of it. Some of these West Indians know a thing or two. (*Distant chants of* '*Stop Rustication!', 'Stop Rustication!'*

Har. Are they shouting 'Stop Rustication'?

Wil. Yes.

Har. Yes. Nasty thing, that rustications.

Wil. How do you mean?

Har. Used to be a lot of it about, like foot and mouth.

Wil. Yes, too much foot in the mouth can lead to rustication.

Har. We used to get lectured about it from the CO. But they cleared it all up.

Wil. How?

Har. Wholesale slaughter. Then they re-stock with new young kids what haven't been infected.

Wil. Why are they trying to stop it again, then?

Har. Must be them foreign fellers bringing it back. They fellers from across the seas are much more prone to the rustications than we are.

Wil. They'd better get 'em all out quickly, then.

Har. Yes. Nasty thing, that rustications. Gets under your hair shirt.

Wil. (*Still thinking about the game*). What does?

Har. (*Emphatically*). The rustications! Makes you itch all over and come out in scabs. (*Pause*). Scabs often come with the rustications. (*Scratches himself melodramatically*). If you irritate 'em they get worse. Bleedin' scabs is the worst of all.

Wil. What do you do, then?

Har. You have to take your trousers down and be victimised.

Wil. What, on the lawn?

Har. No, of course not. They do it in private.

Wil. (*Not quite understanding*). They do it in private?

Har. So long as you're an adult and they have your consent, you can do it in private.

Wil. What?

Har. What? Why don't you get a new battery for your infernal machine, Willmot? You don't expect me to shout at my age?

Wil. If I were your age, *I'd* shout at it.

Har. What's the point? You wouldn't get any younger, it wouldn't go away.

Wil. (*Suddenly remembering that his question has not been answered*).

What do you get done in private?

Har. (*Absent-mindedly*) Lots of people get done in private nowadays. (*Sighs*). Used to be done in public in my day, with everyone joining in.

Wil. What do they do?

Har. Well, first of all they all get the needle…

Wil. (*Interrupting*) That's not surprising, all out there on the lawn with their trousers down.

Har. (*Somewhat testily*) I'm talking about one of them hyperbolic needles.

Wil. (*Baffled*) Hyper what?

Har. Bolic. But it doesn't hurt so much if you've got some good mates to give you a 'and where it 'urts most afterwards.

(*Distant chants of 'Ho! Ho! Ho Chi Minh!', 'Ho! Ho! Ho Chi Minh' followed by scattered applause*).

What's happening now? Is someone out?

Wil. Must be, Ho Cheem's gone in… (*He is interrupted by distant chants of 'Out! Out! LBJ!', 'Out! Out! LBJ!'*)

Yes, that's it. Ho Cheem's in because L. B. Jay's out. Must be a popular feller to be so well known. Skipper, I shouldn't wonder.

(*A lone voice from the far distance shouts 'Balls!'*)

Hello, they've lost the ball.

(*Renewed shouting, mostly incoherent. The words 'Never!', 'Sit down!', 'Strike!' are picked out from a background of babble*).

I think the game's over.

Har. About time, too. Everybody else must be bored stiff.

Curtain

And so, boys and girls, with our hands on our hearts and our hearts in our boots (a wonderful man, that Professor Barnard), the plaintive song of the woozlum bird echoing up a thousand trouser-legs and our ship sinking slowly in the west, we wave a gentle farewell to our old wise acres of Sussex. As we put them back in their boxes for the night, we leave you to the exultant clamour of horns accompanying a fanfare of strumpets. Remember, he who laughs last probably hasn't seen the joke, or, as the French 'ave 'eet (and who among us doesn't?), 'si le chapeau vous fîte, on le pût'.

And now – Lights! Action! Music! Take your partners for a St Vitus' Dance!'

March 1968

And One Final 'Postscript' To Send You on Your Way:

When Goldilocks wanted to trace her family history, she was much quicker than other people.

It takes a lot of time to trace all our ancestors and forebears. Goldilocks was lucky. She only had threebears.

Goodnight.
And goodbye!